Cracking the Camouflage Ceiling

*Faith Persistence and Progress in the Army Chaplaincy
During the Early Integration of Women in the Military*

Chaplain (Colonel) Janet Yarlott Horton
US Army (Ret)

Hawthorne Publishing
Carmel, Indiana

Copyright © 2017 Chaplain (Colonel) Janet Yarlott Horton, US Army (Ret)

All Rights Reserved. No part of this book may be reproduced or copied in any manner without the written permission of the publisher.

ISBN: 978-0-9963949-5-6

Photos are from the author's collection or taken by army photographers whose credits cannot at this late date be confirmed. Cover photo: Army Chief of Chaplains Matthew Zimmerman presents the Meritorious Service Medal in 1993 to Chaplain Horton.

Author's Note

I would like to thank my husband Jeff Harvey for supporting me through this long road to publishing a book. I couldn't have done it alone. I was initially encouraged by George Spitzer and others who would approach me at talks and urge me to "write a book." Nancy and Art Baxter of Hawthorne Publishing became the instrument for fulfilling that inspired desire.

None of these things could have happened without the love and inspiration of my dad, Richard Yarlott, constantly expressed. Lee Harvath, Carolyn Petersen and Gary and Carol Sondheimer selflessly offered their time and expertise as I wrote. I can't thank them all enough!

Hawthorne Publishing, 15601 Oak Road,
Carmel, IN 46033
Contact us at Hawthornepub.com
317-867-5183

INTRODUCTION

The Lord is my shepherd; I shall not want. Psalm 23

"…[W]e cannot be too grateful nor too humble…"
　　　　　　　　　　　　Mary Baker Eddy (*Miscellany*) 134:5–8)

I remember walking up to the Pentagon in 1989 for my first day in the army chief of chaplains office. Looking at that impressive five-sided building, its cold gray limestone silhouetted against the Potomac skyline, I realized my life was about to change significantly. It's a day like that when you think about how you got there. I was there because I was just one of the women who chose to be a part of the "birth of a new idea." In the mid-1970s the Women's Army Corps (WAC) was eliminated, and the army was directed to integrate women into the regular force. The chaplain corps was one of the very last branches in the army to yield to that directive.

Giving birth is a particularly appropriate comparison for women's integration because it's an experience distinctly unique to and borne by women. Many people had "labor pains" with the idea of women serving, and in the more literal sense, it wasn't until the early 1980s that the policy that military women wouldn't be allowed to bear children was overturned. I was reminded of that analogy each time a commander would find out his new chaplain replacement was a woman and would refuse her sight unseen. It seemed all too much like a dad who found out that the new baby was a girl, not a boy, and expressed his disappointment openly. Fortunately, those types of dads are few and far between!

When I look back on those early days, I recall how progress came only at a very dear price. Yet, the progress did come—a step at a time, and we were all honored to be a part of it.

What helped me immensely was rising above the human sense to a more spiritual sense of progress. Someday a woman will rise to the highest place of distinction in the Army Chaplain Corps. Perhaps on that day, she and others will recognize that accomplishment was not only an individual accomplishment but a collective accomplishment as well. On that day we would all stand, hand in hand, marking the years of ministry invested in breaking that gender barrier and camouflage ceiling.

In my recollections I have tried to include significant events that were moving, challenging, and uplifting as I grew into my calling. I've grouped them into categories that link them to the lessons learned. I claim no credit for the words that often came to mark the day, but I was blessed to listen and hear God telling me how to proceed. There is certainly wisdom in the Book of Psalms as it reminds us "we spend our years as a tale that is told."

My hope would be that this text could record that I tried to live my beliefs at least according to my best light at those moments. If others can benefit from my experiences and catch even a glimmer of what the early women attempted to do, then perhaps others will recognize, if nothing else, that they were humble beginnings on the road to the equitable treatment of women serving in the Army Chaplain Corps. The early experiences had a gravity to them that felt akin to "taking the front rank" in military formations and operations. You often felt like you were in the crosshairs of the debate on women's rights and responsibilities. I felt honored to be a part of that measure of progress towards equal opportunity in the ministry.

PREFACE
THE MIRACLE OF THE MILITARY CHAPLAINCY

Few people understand the dynamics of the military chaplaincy. It is a venerable and valuable institution in our military and in our democracy. The inspiration of faith on the front lines and in all parts of military service safeguards and strengthens and is indeed a bulwark to our national efforts.

The First Amendment may rightfully be considered one miracle of American democracy. The genius of the military chaplaincy has been its ability to provide comprehensive, continuous religious support to service members, families, and authorized civilians without establishing a state religion. Even more miraculously, the chaplaincies somehow manage to do this by the hard work of clergy resources based only on the number of military commanders who choose to designate a personnel authorization for a chaplain in their military units. Military chaplains provide the same level of support to families as they do to Department of Defense (DoD) civilians—who actually outnumber service members—without any additional authorizations for chaplains.

In all America's conflicts clergy have served effectively and offered inspiration and comfort. Ministers accompanied Continental forces opposing Britain in the Revolutionary War. Reverend James Caldwell, as a Presbyterian minister traveling with troops from the colonies through major battles, was such an inspiration that the British offered a reward for his capture. "The Rebel Priest" gave his life in service to his country before he could see its independence realized. Congress appointed chaplains for each brigade in 1777.

The Civil War saw chaplains accompanying regiments, and then brigades, for both North and South. Reverend Archibald Adams, for instance, again a Presbyterian minister, was considered the "angel" of the Seventieth Indiana regiment and accompanied them throughout the war, one of thousands of clergymen chaplains for battlefield and camp.

Today's modern military chaplaincy exists because General Pershing sent a cablegram to the Sixty-Fifth Congress. In their Second Session, in Senate Bill 2917 Section 15 dated December 3, 1917, Pershing's recommendations were adopted as the original requirements for military chaplains. The cablegram stated that military chaplains should be "duly accredited" by some religious denomination or organization and that they should "be of good standing therein." A more recent landmark ruling came as the result of law students who filed a suit questioning the constitutionality of the chaplaincy. On January 22, 1985, in *Katcoff v. Marsh*, all three judges of the Second Circuit Court determined the army chaplaincy was constitutional.

The military chaplaincy differs from local pastoral work because the goal of the chaplain's work is to meet the needs of a tremendously diverse number of persons of faith rather than only those of a specific denomination or belief structure. Military chaplains perform worship and sacramental services for those whose faith is identical or similar to their own and for anyone desiring to participate in the chapel service. Chaplains then coordinate to provide for the diverse worship needs of other people in their unit or military installation. This requires coordination and cooperation with other military chaplains of greatly varied traditions who are a part of the chaplain team at that location.

While the military can train a person to be a combatant service member, a mechanic, a pilot, a cook, or a personnel specialist, it has no authority to credential or educate the officers who choose to serve in the three professional branches: The Judge Advocate General Corps, the Medical Corps, and the Chaplain Corps. The military requires professional officers to complete the required postgraduate level education and certification by a professional organization in order to apply to serve in the armed forces. The military looks to the American Bar Association to certify an attorney, or the American Medical Association to validate a doctor's credentials. For the same reasons the military must look to religious organizations to certify religious ministry professionals.

Because the American religious landscape has exponentially diversified in the last few decades, the clergy who make up the chaplaincy represent a very delicate balance of major faith groups and traditions. Our nation contains over two thousand traditions, and it is impossible for every tradition to be represented in the military chaplaincies. Religious organizations that wish to lend their ministry professionals to the military are required to register with the Department of Defense. They must agree to meet the military requirements for the professional branches in order to nominate their candidates for service in the armed forces. Registered religious organizations then appoint an endorsing agent to certify the credentials of their ministry professionals for the DoD. The number of religious organizations registered with the DoD to provide chaplains has multiplied from fifty in the early 1900s to over two hundred in the new century. Christianity, Judaism, Islam, and Buddhism are the major faith groups currently represented. More than two hundred Christian churches have ministry professionals serving with the military.

Providing religious services and meeting the greatly varied religious needs of service members and their families is a complicated task. Whether the religious services provided are acceptable to any person is a matter of individual faith. Both the clergyperson providing the religious support and the congregants receiving the support subjectively and individually determine whether they can participate in either multi-faith group or multi-denominational worship experiences. The wisdom of the Koran would apply to this aspect of chaplain services. It notes that there is no compulsion in religion. The chaplains and service members all understand no one can be forced to attend any type of religious services. Atheists have also requested representation in the military chaplaincies to make sure broader arrays of beliefs are respected.

The National Conference on Ministry to the Armed Forces (NCMAF) is a voluntary civilian affiliation of endorsing agents who meet annually to discuss current issues about religious support in the military. The endorsing agents determine the flow of clergy from their civilian structure into the military departments. NCMAF has no official relationship to the DoD, but it holds great informal power. The chaplaincies could not function without the religious ministry professionals from the organizations who make up NCMAF.

Because the beliefs of service members are extremely diverse, the chaplaincy is only successful in its demanding mission by also combining and mobilizing lay resources. These lay ministers may be fellow service members, local civilian volunteers, or representatives from local religious organizations near the military installations. The military chapels then provide the volunteer lay ministers worship space and the opportunity to augment the military chaplains' delivery of individual religious support to members of their specific denomination or differing faith groups.

Because some military members have worshiped in Protestant chapels or in deployed or remote settings, they often don't think of themselves as having a particular Christian denomination. Some may not identify with an exclusive faith group. In surveys roughly 25 percent of all service members select the ambiguous category of "no preference" to describe their worship needs. This category by no means only represents those who aren't religious. Many are Christians who are comfortable worshiping with any other Christians. Some service members may mean that they are comfortable in multi-faith worship. And still others would say they choose that category because they are not involved with formal religion and yet consider themselves to be spiritual. To complicate comprehensive support, no data is collected on family members who may not share the preferences of the service member who is their sponsor.

New chaplains just entering the military begin providing religious support while assigned to units of about eight hundred soldiers. These battalion chaplains provide individual ministry wherever their unit of assignment is working. The unit members consider the new officer as *their* chaplain because that is the person who makes the ten-mile road march with them and deploys with the unit if they leave their installation. He or she is the clergyperson they've come to know. The bond is usually strong and one of great trust. The chaplain may provide individual counseling, encourage the new person to complete the long morning run, or simply walk the long, lonesome trail with them in a combat zone. They also coordinate for all the people in their unit to have an opportunity to worship in the manner they choose. The familiar staff chaplain is the person the unit members turn to when they are troubled or need an answer of peace about their work or life challenges that they face. They may bring their family members with them or a co-worker who is involved in a work issue. Unit chaplains' duties are as diverse as people's needs, and service members often call for a chaplain beyond the normal working hours. The chaplains involved with military units could receive a call in the middle of the night if there is a hospitalized service member or a crisis occurs with the service member and their family.

It is not uncommon during training for a soldier to have a crisis, or to do something dangerous or threatening, or to simply become paralyzed with fear. The chaplain may be called in to calm and stabilize the person and talk them through the crisis. These are leadership roles commonly associated and assumed by chaplains who are able to develop credibility and confidence in the eyes of their fellow service members. Some soldiers may even find in the middle of a war zone that they want to rethink the meaning of life.

Chaplains provide various forms of grief counseling. They are tasked with the solemn duty of notifying a service member when their parent, grandparent, or other family member has passed on. Chaplains are a vital part of every step involved in the death of a service member. They are part of the team that notifies the family when a service member dies on duty. From the time that prayer or last rites are administered, to the ramp ceremonies during the transport of the body of the service member, the conduct of the unit memorial services, graveside burial, and military honors, a chaplain provides the appropriate prayer and rites to meet the service member's declared religious preferences and the family's requests.

Chaplains also support service members during the happier times of their lives. They may christen a baby, baptize a new believer, perform a wedding, or conduct the celebration when a couple wishes to renew their vows on an anniversary. The chaplain is there for service members through all the varied seasons of their life journey.

The chaplain is also a member of the commander's staff and advises the commander on the morale in the unit or any issues that may have moral implications. Because chaplains counsel people of various ranks, they may see a trend in the number of times a specific issue of leadership or conduct arises. The chaplain may alert the command to the overall concern, but they cannot use specific names or violate the counselee's confidentiality. Yet, there are times that the service members themselves ask the chaplain to help initiate bringing a harassment charge or a questionable action to the commander for correction or legal action if required.

Chaplains carefully monitor post-traumatic stress disorder (PTSD) concerns in their units. They conduct family retreats prior to deployments and when the families are reunited after deployments. They can provide PTSD counseling for individual soldiers and family members and help everyone transition in a productive and supportive environment.

As chaplains progress in rank and are assigned to larger, higher-level commands, they begin to assume leadership roles. Besides the individual ministry they will always provide, they become the supervisors for chaplains assigned to subordinate units in their commander's area of responsibility. They mentor, counsel, and train subordinate chaplains and chaplain assistants. The chaplain could be a part of shaping new standing operating procedures or policy that affects families or service members. Chaplains advise the commander on training before deployments that helps families and service members address the stress and changes that accompany such long-term separations. At this higher staff level, chaplains may have a larger picture and knowledge of repetitive concerns that would not be as visible to each individual commander.

The highest-ranking chaplains advise commanders as staff officers at the army's high level commands or at the Department of Defense staff groups supervised by generals in the Pentagon. When a change in army policy has an impact on the religious rights of service members, a chaplain advises the secretary of the army or the secretary of defense, as appropriate. The chaplain helps assess how to minimize the impact on the specific religious rights that would be restricted in such cases as when worship or religious practices conflict with operational tempo or locations, the revocation of waivers of immunization based on religious beliefs, the impact wearing of required religious apparel has on the normal uniform regulations, etc. Case law that historically supported restriction of free exercise of religion includes practices, rites, or observances that present a clear and present danger (i.e., membership in extremist/hate groups); unlawful activities (criminal or civil); or worship including practices that are considered a violation of fire, safety, good order, or discipline.

At all levels of the military our chaplains selflessly serve both God and their country. Rarely do they receive appreciation for their extraordinary contributions, and yet rarely do they seek such notice. It is with great gratitude that I served, and the bond that I feel with both active and fellow retired chaplains still moves me.

Assignment History

    1976 Fort Wadsworth, New York; Chaplain Officer Basic Course
    1976–1979 Fort Sill, Oklahoma, Fourth Battalion Thirty-First Infantry Battalion Chaplain
    1979–1980 Second Infantry Division, Camp Casey, Korea; Brigade Chaplain
    1980–1981 Fort Monmouth, New Jersey, Chaplain Officer Advanced Course/Instructor
    1981–1982 Fort Ord, California, Headquarters Battalion Chaplain
    1983–1984 Defense Language Institute Chapel, Presidio of Monterey, California
    1984–1985 Stanford University; MA Religious Studies
    1985–1989 Fort Harrison, Indiana, US Soldier Support Center, Combined Arms Dept. Ethics/Leadership Instructor
    1989–1993 Pentagon, Chief of Chaplains Office; Career Management Officer
    1993–1994 First Armored Division, Germany; Division Chaplain
    1994–1995 Carlisle Barracks, Pennsylvania, Army War College
    1995–1997 Fort Jackson, South Carolina, US Army Chaplain School, Director of Training
    1997–2000 Heidelberg, Germany, V Corps Headquarters Corps Chaplain
    2000–2003 Pentagon, Armed Forces Chaplains Board Exec. Director
    2003–2004 Fort Belvoir, Virginia, Intelligence and Security Command, Major Command Chaplain

CHAPTER 1
PUTTING ON THE WHOLE ARMOR OF GOD

Yea, though I walk through the valley of the shadow of death,
I will fear no evil: for thou art with me.
"The whole armour of God" (Ephesians 6:13)
"God…thou hast made the heaven and the earth by thy great power and stretched out arm, and there is nothing too hard for thee:"
(Jeremiah 32:17)

My heritage, which would play such an important part in my groundbreaking career story, unfolded both out of my close family background and at God's direction. I was the second daughter of Dick and Peggy Yarlott, born in Crystal, Michigan. My two baby brothers were very much a part of my growing love for sports, and we were very close. My older sister and I were both considered girls too smart for our day and age. My dad was a salesman and inventor, and my mom was a strict but loving caretaker.

We found Christian Science when my dad and mom both experienced striking healings when I was in grade school. The first time my mom let us kids go to church with Dad, to First Church of Christ, Scientist, Alma, Michigan, I remember feeling a deep sense of peace and joy that I was where I belonged. Edna Marshall Dill, a Christian Science practitioner, also healed my younger brother when doctors were unable to stop his dehydration when he was a baby. Whenever my dad and I would go to her home, we inevitably felt a profound loving kindness in everything she did. Through Mrs. Dill I developed a deep appreciation for the uplifting effect that studying our weekly Christian Science Bible lesson had on my spiritual growth and preparation for meeting whatever the day's events unfolded.

We moved to Oklahoma for a brief six months when I was eleven and then moved on to Ankeny, Iowa, a suburb of Des Moines. I was equally blessed there to have wonderful Sunday School teachers who helped me understand how to pray for specific challenges and to constantly affirm the wondrous blessing each day included. Because of the clearer understanding of the infinite nature of God's love and care that I was feeling from studying the Bible and the writings of Mary Baker Eddy, I was able to overcome a severe sense of shyness. That helped me develop a sense of confidence grounded on understanding that it was God who had blessed me with the intelligence I expressed.

I loved school and through prayer was able to attend a church college in Iowa. I always thought I would be a teacher and was completing a year of graduate studies at the University of Iowa when our church contacted me and asked me to interview for our Military Chaplain Training Program in Boston. In 1972 women were just being given the opportunity to serve in the U.S. military rather than in limited ways in auxiliary corps. I became the first woman to serve for The First Church of Christ, Scientist as an army chaplain in 1976. There were two other women who had come into the army chaplaincy, each as the only female in her respective Chaplain Officer basic course in 1974 and 1975. Our 1976 basic course was the third class to include women. All of us women chaplains from that time were from different denominations, and we faced challenges that were both differing and the same.

In the mid-1970s I began my military career, and despite the preponderance of predictions women would "never make it" in the Chaplain Corps, we all chose to put on the whole armor of God in the army. In the days ahead it was the caring family values I learned as a child, the marvelous education God had provided for me, and a deep and certain sense of God's calling me to "comfort his people" that would be the foundation for my ministry, which I now understood would be in the army. I was realistic enough to know that our whole society was only gradually acknowledging women as the equals of men and that there would be stereotypes to overcome, and yet I knew I would be safe and secure in God's keeping. It was increasingly clear when He "sends us" to minister, we do not walk alone, and that lifted any fear that merely human opinions and beliefs could stand in the way of true spiritual progress.

For anyone entering the military it would be common to think about the idea of armor. The issue of safety is frequently at the forefront of your thought. As a chaplain you are a non-combatant, but you do wear body armor because so many places you go could be dangerous. What I didn't realize was how dangerous it would be to break new ground in public thought. The realization that I needed spiritual armor hit me early in my seminary training. It was great that my job during seminary was nighttime security in Back Bay Boston. It expanded my concept of praying daily for my safety. I learned so much, and those lessons helped me meet some of the subsequent safety challenges while serving as an army chaplain.

Safety is a term that can have many meanings and nuances. During the early years I found that expanding roles for women was a very threatening idea for those in society who weren't welcoming the change. I had to learn, step by step, that my safety was in God's hands. From my study of Bible stories, it was clear to me that nothing was too hard for God, omnipotent good. I often reviewed how powerful God's hand was in the lives of Daniel, Ruth, and Jesus. It was obvious that Biblical figures faced many fiery ordeals. I learned that the furnace refined and purified the gold in character. The harder part was to grasp how Shadrach, Meshach, and Abednego came through that ordeal without even the smell of smoke on their clothes.

When I returned from my summer internship with our active duty chaplains, my church trainer and supervisor asked me how I viewed the resistance I had encountered. He seemed somewhat surprised that the resistance had been so overt. I showed him how I had been praying during the toughest parts and that the following ideas from the Bible came to me. What I was experiencing seemed similar to the type of resistance Christians felt when they encountered Saul before he had seen the bright light of the Christ truth Jesus embodied. Saul truly thought he was guarding the law and truth, as he perceived it. However, when he was converted on his journey to Damascus, he heard the reproof, recorded in Acts 9, which shows Jesus saying, "it is hard for thee to kick against the pricks."

A radical change was taking place in thought across America. The restricted role of women in our society was being challenged. For some these were not just baby steps but leaps of faith. What occurred to me was that John 1:5 was applicable: "And the light shineth in darkness; and the darkness comprehended it not." The blinding light Saul experienced when he encountered the Christ did, in the end, change his heart and lead him to a place of higher understanding. I felt the important result was the changed heart in the end. That was what I needed to focus on rather than the initial resistance, no matter how severe or pronounced it was. I have always felt that the humble beginnings of any new truth mirrors that journey. The first persons who attempt to change thought about an entrenched belief will find that even the self-righteous who initially resisted the change as Paul did often progressed and even encouraged others to make the same recognitions and supported the advance in attitude in the end.

My duties as a military chaplain evolved over the course of my service. The chaplaincy as a whole has actually evolved and continues to evolve today, as the demands of the service change. In those first days we women were few, but I think we were strong. The female chaplains who were pioneering a new trend across the military services did so as individuals, occasionally coming across each other but having no real time or funding to meet as a group. At those times we were together, army women chaplains compared experiences, and it was of great comfort and furthered our friendship. However, most of the time we were on our own with God and some friends wherever we found them.

And so it began, with faith as a guide and firmness in the face of misguided opposition as a light. I moved on, and with those guideposts day by day to progress and fulfillment and service to my country, and I hope, to others. I would serve for twenty-eight years on active duty, and I would always recall arriving and finding challenges—and in prayer I'd turn over my life to God to meet them. I had, after all, as I stood at that climactic moment of active duty, already proven to myself over and over that with the whole armor of God, one can "stand your ground, after you have done everything, to stand" (New International Version). These few moments of my history that follow show how impervious that whole armor (as we now spell it) is.

Recognizing that God polices the universe and that insures our safety

In 1974 I worked night security to pay for my expenses in seminary. Near the end of an evening, on one of our TV monitors, my security supervisor saw a couple being assaulted. I was told to assist because the perpetrators were beating the man. The Boston Police Department (BPD) had been notified and two cruisers were on the way.

I've always been convinced there's a Bible story applicable to anything we could possibly experience. The parable of the Good Samaritan in Luke, of the traveler who fell among thieves, came to my thought. I knew I couldn't just pass by without aiding the couple in need. I prayed to understand clearly what God wanted me to do. I knew if he brought me there, He had a purpose for it. It became clear that I wasn't there to physically intervene. That would only increase the level of violence in an already violent situation. My approach was to pray to understand that violence didn't exist in God's creation. The first chapter of Genesis affirms God saw everything he created and "it was very good." I knew I couldn't be anywhere that God wasn't already there when I arrived.

I calmly walked up to the three men assaulting the couple and explained that we'd called the BPD. I suggested they wait right there and we'd have the police cars there in a moment. Gratefully, the audacity of what I said caused them to stop attacking the couple. They looked at me in utter astonishment. This caused two of them to run off down the alley. It was almost laughable because they ran straight into a BPD cruiser at the end of the alley.

The third man simply ran away toward the Boson Back Bay Sheraton lobby. Rather than taking it upon myself to restrain him, I was just running behind him while broadcasting our current location on my hand-held radio. We ran through the Prudential Shopping Center. He ran into the subway and out the other end onto the street. I continued to run behind him for about twenty minutes, and with each new turn I would broadcast our current location. Finally, a BPD car pulled up beside the panting man, who now seemed exhausted. He exclaimed, "Just take me!" No one else was hurt. The criminals basically apprehended themselves.

If we are alert not to take matters into our own hands, such malicious actions in the end betray and destroy themselves. Our part is largely to pray and follow God's directions. Calmly waiting on Him allows God to orchestrate the perfect events to resolve any problem. "All power is given unto our Lord, On Him we place reliance," as Martin Luther's majestic hymn states.

Chaplain (Colonel) Janet Yarlott Horton, US Army (Ret)

The Arizona desert—Face to face with coyotes and men's malice

Early in my military career, in 1977, stationed at Fort Sill, I found that I was repeatedly being sent to be the token woman in chaplain conferences. At a retreat center near Phoenix, Arizona, I joined the other chaplains for their early morning physical training. The guys were discussing running out to a foothill behind our retreat center. The male chaplains cautioned me it was too far, but I explained I'd been running six to nine miles a day with my infantry unit at Fort Sill. Reluctantly they agreed I could try to do the run. None of us were desert people, so we weren't familiar with the illusion of distances. After about three miles of running in the barren desert occasionally dotted with prickly cacti, it became clear it was probably ten times the distance it appeared to be. We also realized we had to run back! When we turned around we were a considerable distance from any populated areas.

I had been praying to take my mind off the length of the run. All of a sudden, I realized that I was alone and wondered where the guys went. I looked around to see a pack of hungry coyotes were out looking for their morning breakfast. They began to growl and circle me. When the lead dog growled and moved in, the others would close in tighter.

Because the thought came to me of how much I loved animals, especially the dogs we had when I was a child, I never remember feeling any sense of fear. A wonderful Bible lesson that day from the thirteenth and fourteenth chapters of Numbers had been about those who went in to spy out the land of Canaan. Some gave an evil report and said it was a land that devoured its people and was inhabited by giants. But Caleb gave a good and true report. Right where the men he journeyed with saw a dangerous situation, Caleb saw a land that flowed with milk and honey and felt that the people were able to possess it. Having been "praying without ceasing," I felt very prepared during the run. I did, however, sense a "gravity" to the situation as the circling coyotes began to close in. Next, I recalled the Bible account of Daniel in the lions' den. Daniel's heart was pure and there was no fear, animalistic tendency, nor hate that he'd been thrown into the lions' den. There was nothing impure in his heart or mind for the lions to feed on.

Turning away from the picture in front of me, I prayed to hear the still small voice of God's Word for this situation. What came to me was "get down and speak to the lead dog." So I got down on one knee. When I knelt, the lead coyote lay down. Then all the other coyotes did also and became very attentive. What happened literally was an example of Jesus's instructions to "preach the gospel to every creature."

Starting with the first chapter of Genesis, "In the beginning," I told them that God created the heaven and the earth, the sea and all that therein is. He divided the light from the darkness. He created every creeping thing upon the earth. He saw everything He had made, and behold it was very good. I was also praying with this idea from the Christian Science textbook, *Science and Health with Key to the Scriptures*, by Mary Baker Eddy, that "All of God's creatures, moving in the harmony of Science, are harmless, useful, indestructible" (514:28–30).

I said to the lead coyote, "You have a purpose, but it's not to harm me. And I have a purpose, and it's not to harm you. We need to be about our Father's business, but it's not here." Then I said, "You need to go now." I waved my hand upward and then pointed out into the desert. The lead coyote popped up and took off, and all the other coyotes followed him, trotting away.

It was then that I realized the men had seen the coyotes coming and had sprinted ahead. Some had climbed a brick wall that was to be the entrance to a new development. Others were up a couple of trees nearby. When they knew the coyotes were gone, they climbed down and began to sort of "fess up." Some admitted they had been holding anger and resentment about women being forced into the chaplaincy. Some said they didn't feel women had earned the opportunity to go to these conferences. Another chaplain said he never thought our church should have been allowed to have military chaplains. Although it seemed as if there was a lot of ravenous thought, it had no voice or authority in the end.

This incident gave me the opportunity to share with them that women chaplains didn't want to be star-spangled Barbie dolls either, but we had to execute orders we were given. It was senior chaplains who insisted on a token woman at all conferences. We all achieved a new level of understanding, and they expressed appreciation for the new insights

A number of the chaplains left remarking that this was the most amazing thing they'd ever seen. One man commented that if I could preach to wild dogs and they'd listen to me…well, that probably meant soldiers would, too. We all got a big laugh out of that and it took the edge off the events.

In the military we're very fond of saying, "the bottom line is…" God was opening the petals of a holy purpose as women entered the chaplaincy, and these challenging events were occurring for the healing of misperceptions, anger, or hatred. If these events occur, then the bottom line is that they occur to bless us. God had brought all the right elements together. Often the events he uses defy every predetermined expectation you could have.

When I shared this experience with other women chaplains at a meeting, their responses surprised me. They were incensed about the men not coming to my rescue. I told them that God was protecting us all, and it was probably better that they didn't needlessly endanger themselves or escalate the situation. No doubt, they, too, felt reassured that God guides us all.

One of the women humorously asked if I thought I was in more danger from the coyotes on the ground or the "dawgs" in the trees. Everyone roared when she put it that way. I thought for a moment and assured them all that it was because I knew I was in no danger from the coyotes on the ground or God's children in the trees, that I was there to tell them of the event. That experience invariably comes to thought when I read Ezekiel 34:28, "And they shall no more be a prey to the heathen, neither shall the beast of the land devour them; but they shall dwell safely, and none shall make them afraid."

Persons of interest

It wouldn't be honest if I didn't admit that in the early years there were some pretty tough challenges for women chaplains. The most astounding early recognition I had was the realization that not all the resistance was from military men or male chaplains: women were a part of the resistance!

One civilian woman deceived a maid in the Bachelor Officer Quarters (BOQ) and convinced her she needed to enter my BOQ and did not need to be escorted. She pretended to be returning something and poured bleach on my tropical fish. They were the first mated pair of Gold Angelfish ever bred in captivity. My dad was so proud of his accomplishment that he had had them delivered to me by a friend coming to Oklahoma. I have always had a very soft heart for animals. I often thought I'd have preferred she poured the bleach on me. At least I could have defended myself.

Even after moving off the military post to an apartment in Lawton, I still found large amounts of my clothing, jewelry, and home furnishing items were disappearing. Then one day as I drove to work I noticed a vehicle sitting close to the road in a parking lot. I watched the driver pull a stocking mask over his face. He proceeded at full speed to ram his car at mine. I was driving a small sports car at the time and it had very responsive steering, enabling me to swerve off the road and down into a dry creek bed. It brought to mind two other very recent times drivers had swerved at my vehicle. Before that, I just chalked it up to bad drivers. I couldn't write this third instance off to that excuse.

It was necessary to report this incident to the police and my senior chaplain. Because of the amount of incidents that had occurred, the supervisory chaplains, the Fort Sill commanders, and the police recommended that I execute my pending travel orders to Korea a little early.

Just before I left, a man in an identical make, model, and detailing as my car was run off the road within a mile of where the man attempted to ram my car. I was grateful when I found out he was not hurt badly, even though his car was totaled. The police were investigating as I left for Princeton, where the women chaplains were meeting for the second army women chaplains conference. There would be a few more curious occurrences after I reached Korea.

"Thou shalt not bear false witness" nor make false reports: Still safe

Shortly after I arrived in Korea in 1979, I was called to the military police station and asked why I had been making false police reports. Whoever was really making them, trying to get me in trouble, wasn't very astute. The false reports were always made when I could verify that I was in a public place and I hadn't even been near a phone. This, however, seemed all too much like the strange events at Fort Sill that were the very reason for my early move to Korea.

Just a few days later a person came to my office. Most military people are very aware that what you say to a chaplain is privileged communication. The individual asked me some questions that were related to cases I was involved with at Fort Sill. The person referred to the false police reports and mentioned a certain group of people who had been watching me and also referred to other, more questionable events. I was told if I could assure this person that I was no threat to the group mentioned, everything would stop.

While affirming that chaplains had clerical privilege, I also stated that

I had no need or desire to intrude into any person's private life or make judgments about their life choices or affiliations. I emphasized that I treated everyone the same, and considered all people as children of the one heavenly Father and only creator of the universe. Yet, I wanted to be clear that I didn't care if a person was a "kangaroo"; criminal behavior was a totally different matter. The visitor relaxed and seemed comforted by my lightness in distinguishing between kangaroos and criminals. I told the person that I did want to make it perfectly clear that criminal behavior was not only illegal, but more importantly unethical. I was assured that we had an understanding. After that I don't remember any other unexplainable happenings occurring during that tour.

A spiritual position of attention

In the mid-1980s a sergeant was sexually harassing female soldiers at our military installation. He had kicked in the side of one woman's car. Two other women also told me they made formal written complaints. I talked to the company commander, a young captain. He was simply allowing the complaint packet to sit in his inbox. After a reasonable amount of time, I pressed the captain to act or I would take the issue to his boss, the battalion commander.

The sergeant, whom I'd never met, was not happy that I was supporting the sexual harassment investigation. On a very busy day he barged into the chapel annex through a sea of people waiting to see me, loudly proclaiming, "I want to talk to you." In the class B uniform a nametag was optional, and he was not wearing one. I assumed this must be the sergeant in the complaints because he was so aggressive. He began to come at me, poking me in the chest with his finger. Because he was a non-commissioned officer (NCO) and I was a commissioned officer, if you know anything about the military, you'd know we were in No-No Land. He was punching me so hard that he was literally forcing me backward.

My non-commissioned officer in-charge (NCOIC) was throwing down the phone and my specialist was coming over her desk, intending to physically restrain the man. To protect everyone involved, I turned to God with my whole heart. I was really in a position of attention, spiritually. It came to me to simply put my hand up to stop my chaplain assistants from becoming involved. Then, another thought came very vividly: "He's a service member. Bring him to a position of attention."

With distinct authority in my voice, I said, "Sergeant! Come to a position of attention." Every indication prior to that said he was completely out of control. Yet, the moment I ordered him to a position of attention, he stopped in his tracks. He came to a position of attention, and no one had to touch him.

I was struck by the picture of how powerful a discipline that must have been for him. Regardless of the fact his world, as he knew it, was being questioned and things seemed to be spinning out of control, still he responded like a good non-commissioned officer. Everything else in his world stopped. I told him with great authority that he had disgraced the uniform he was wearing. Then I directed him to immediately report to his commander. I told both my assistants not to talk to each other but to write up statements describing what had just occurred. For publically assaulting an officer, the sergeant was reduced in rank. He was also identified for orders that would move him to a new duty station.

When I returned from a meeting a few days later, my chaplain assistant told me not to go into my office. The sergeant was in the chapel annex sitting in a chair, red faced and shaking with anger. He had told the assistant he was going to kill me. I knew it would be important for everyone involved to be very wise and asked God to put the words in my mouth that would be needed. Calling the MPs and his commander, I told them to send the 1SGT (first sergeant) and this man's best friend or roommate. The MPs were to wait outside, keeping us in visual contact.

As I entered the chapel annex, he growled a low harsh accusation at me that I was destroying his career. Feeling confident that God could meet this challenge from the sergeant as He had in the first encounter, I asked him calmly if he would come into my office with his friend or the 1SGT and discuss it. He agreed and calmed to a degree. He chose his friend to accompany him.

It came to me to ask him if I had come to his place of duty and threatened him and pushed him. In a very low voice, he reluctantly said, "No." I asked him if I had sexually harassed any of the other service members? He again, very slowly, said, "No." Contrary to his frank admissions, he remained very invested in protecting his career. He continued demanding that I withdraw my statement about the incident. I told him I would never file a statement that I intended to withdraw. However, I told him I would amend it, if he could show me anything in the statement that wasn't true or didn't fairly represent him or the events of that day.

It was so clear to me that only God, expressed as the Truth, could save this man from himself. I believe that Truth is that powerful. I believe it is equal to any situation. It is God that informs the situation when we hold to the truth as He knows it and reveals it to all involved—if we listen.

I talked with him about principle and what had governed his actions. Before he left, he became calm enough to agree that it had been his own actions that had placed him in peril. I reminded him that he would honor the uniform if he would be responsible for his own actions. He left thinking about what I had said without any further disruptive actions.

Shortly after the sergeant left for his new assignment, I went to buy shrimp on my lunch hour at a nearby restaurant on our wharf. As I left, I stopped to give a coin to a tiny monkey who always performed there. As I turned to go to my car, I felt drawn to look up the hill to the expensive hotel that overlooked the bay. A moving van was coming down the hill at what seemed to be a very risky and high rate of speed. I was wondering what it would be doing up that road, as a very upscale hotel was the only thing up there. Then I realized it wasn't going to make the sharp turn at the bottom of the hill. It came straight at me, jumping the curb as it swerved up onto the sidewalk. Being rather athletic, I was able to leap sideways in the air. I landed in a large metal garbage dumpster that sat at the edge of the wharf adjacent to the parking lots. The moving truck scraped the edge of the dumpster, moving it to one side. The driver didn't stop, but hurried out of the wharf area and quickly disappeared down the road.

I was in my class A dress uniform. One of my high heels broke when I pushed off to leap into the dumpster. When I crawled out of the dumpster, I had clumps of garbage on my hair and uniform. I was so shocked I only brushed off the larger pieces and went quickly to my car. The wharf had been rather quiet that day, and only a few people saw what happened.

For quite some time, I'd play the scene over and over in my thought. It seemed surreal. I was never quite certain it wasn't connected somehow to the sergeant's threat that he would kill me. I have no evidence to support that it was or wasn't. I would prefer to think it was just a coincidence. But there had been so many times people had seemed to act in rash and unexplainable ways in those early years. I only mention it because it was one of the few things that really baffled me. And that allowed me to stand firm, with that spiritual protection firmly in place.

"Everlasting arms of love" (Christian Science Hymnal, hymn #53)

An officer who was a friend of mine invited me to take a ride in his newly restored 1952 Austin Healy Bugeye Sprite. The antique car had a low, tight suspension and no seat belts. Even though the road was winding and the car wasn't traveling at a great rate of speed, the right wheels slid off the edge of some new pavement that was unmarked. The old pavement extended a bit more beyond the new addition. The car violently dipped down over the edge. This launched the car into the air directly at a telephone pole.

This all happened in a moment. All I had time to do was hold in my consciousness that I couldn't be separated from God. I knew God was omniscient and would know what to do and was doing it. My only memory was the sense of a hand reaching out and tenderly lifting me and setting me down on a patch of grass. It reminded me of a hymn, "Everlasting arms of Love are beneath, around, above." I had almost no sense of an impact with anything. I felt so loved by God and never felt more certain that my heritage as a child of God was infinite goodness.

Witnesses said the car flipped in the air. The highway patrolman that arrived at the scene refused to believe that I had been a passenger in the car. He just kept repeating, "But you don't have a mark on you." Only after witnesses insisted they had seen me in the car did he enter that fact into the report. The car was totaled. I was concerned for the driver, who was being attended to by EMTs. He had a very different experience and was taken to the military hospital. I kept him in my prayers for the next two weeks. He recovered with no permanent injuries and was discharged in just a few weeks.

I played a tennis match that evening. My opponent, a woman ten years younger than I, said, "I'd have sworn I was playing Chris Evert." I won the match by a considerable margin. For the next two weeks, people at work who knew the driver and me kept asking why I wasn't hurt by the crash. It surprised me a bit that people found it so hard to believe that prayer made a significant difference. I felt so certain that God was willing to help if we made a practice of acknowledging his ability to protect us, no matter what the human circumstances tried to dictate.

A spiritual safety briefing

In 2000 the European V Corps conducted a field training exercise at Grafenwoehr, Germany. The field exercise included eight thousand soldiers and lasted about eight weeks. Because this was a winter season, the soldiers ended up traveling across Germany in icy, snowy road conditions. The soldiers from the stateside reserve division would do so with little or no prior knowledge of the autobahn speeds or conditions. A German division also joined in this massive training opportunity. Because of the weather, the number of participants, and the fact that we had just returned from intensely demanding Balkan missions, the leadership began to express great fear that we would have unusually high numbers of accidental deaths and injuries.

As the corps chaplain I was responsible for the religious support for all the participants for the entire training exercise. I decided to address these fears with all the military chaplains, chaplain assistants, denominational lay leaders, and the priest from the German division. Calling them together for what I termed a spiritual safety briefing, I invited everyone to join together to pray daily for the safety of our soldiers. I suggested that there was no reason that we had to accept there needed to be even a single fatality—IF we would pray daily and specifically for the safety of our soldiers.

I invited them to use the next two days to search their scriptures, hymns, and other sacred texts and come back prepared to share anything they found that constituted assurances and praises of God's power to protect His people. I asked them to confirm for their soldiers and us the scriptural basis for not yielding to fear in such situations. We all agreed to embrace the idea of God's love for his children. They seemed very enthusiastic about such a prospect. At our second meeting people read favorite passages like the 121st or Ninety-First Psalms. Some sang hymns; some read prayers they wrote. It was truly inspiring, and the praise session lasted close to two hours. At the end of the meeting, I reminded them we would do such specific prayer each day, and if there were any particular challenges we would put out a call for dedicated prayer for each case. I briefed the leadership on our commitment to pray daily for the soldiers' safety. They joyfully embraced the idea.

In the corps staff there was a specific section called the Safety Section. At each morning and evening brief, slides were put up detailing the exact number of vehicle accidents, injuries, and deaths. The corps surgeon also had a slide that would detail types and number of cases he'd treated. For the first few days there was nothing. Then the German general fell down in his morning brief and was medically evacuated. His deputy said he was not expected to return because doctors had diagnosed a major challenge. We put out the word for prayer, and by the time the exercise formally started, the German general was back. The leadership was very surprised, and he said the doctors had no medical explanation for why he was back and well so quickly.

Throughout the eight weeks there wasn't a single vehicle or travel-related accident. Our helicopters flew without incident. Soldiers who flew in from the States drove safely from Frankfurt or Munich to Grafenwoehr in very icy conditions. The field exercise progressed and none of the dangers anticipated occurred. The corps surgeon remarked in one briefing that he felt like he was out of business. He hadn't even dispensed so much as a cold packet.

The German general asked me to come to their chapel and address his entire leadership. He wanted them to understand more about the concept of praying specifically about the safety of our soldiers. They particularly loved the idea of being at a position of attention spiritually.

Towards the end of the activities we had to "jump" our main headquarters' elements. The corps needed to maintain more than two hundred functions in a single large tent, while their normal work sections' equipment was loaded onto trucks and a relocation was simulated. Because the huge tent would be packed with soldiers shoulder to shoulder, each person's place was carefully measured in inches. And because the general's staff officers were so impressed with the safety that resulted from the prayer, they refused to continue without their planner chaplain. They vowed they'd make room for his important function.

An incident occurred during the timed dismantling of the headquarters. A soldier got a cable wrapped around his little finger, severing its top half. The predictions were dire, as they supposedly didn't find the finger right away. Then the Medevac helicopter was way late. At the hospital they couldn't locate the needed neurosurgeon immediately. He predicted there would be no way to save the finger. We put out the word for specific prayer. Everyone responded immediately.

Contrary to the dire predictions, the man was back within a two-day period. His finger had been reattached and he had full movement. The only remaining issue was that he might lose the little fingernail—which, of course, would grow back.

The final day the MP who was the security for our classified documents lost control of his weapon. When it hit the ground, the M-16 rifle fired off a live round. The discharged bullet went through the entire tent with the two-hundred-plus people elbow to elbow. The joke at the end of the exercise was that the only fatality was the printer it took out on the opposite end of the tent.

After that our command group always insisted that a chaplain was structured in our Task Forces. Many people with us recognized the Biblical truth that the prayer of the righteous avails much. The fact that this was completely embraced by persons of faith across major faith groups and denominational lines, as well as by our international coalition leadership from Germany, seemed even more astounding. God, the one divine mind, truly united the people on that exercise.

My small part was to simply remind them of the fact that healing is scriptural and is a witness of God's preserving and sustaining power. They naturally began to search their hearts to recall the texts they knew were in their tradition's scriptures.

A prayer that I wrote was published just before the finale of the exercise.
Not One of Them
Lord, a task of great magnitude looms before us!
Yet its promise is a greater sense of unity for having done it together.
And the greatest will be the sense of joy and accomplishment it will bring,
when we see it finished before us.

May your Spirit unite us for just such a work.
Each one of us is needed.
Focus our minds and hearts.
Fill us with the wisdom to see if our haste or hurry
might endanger anyone around us.
Help us to see clearly how our actions may touch others.
May a deep and abiding concern for the well-being of our team
be first and foremost in all we do.
Not one of them needs to fear.

May each one of them know how much they mean to us,

and that they are precious in Your sight.
Each step of the way let us sense Your protecting presence.
We know, beneath Your sheltering wing,
Your ever-watchful eye will guide us.
Not one of them can be outside Your vigilant heart.
And when the task is done, and we thank You for their care,
the greatest joy will be that not one of them was harmed.

"…take unto you the whole armour of God, that ye may be able to withstand in the evil day, and having done all, to stand." That is what has always been, and that is what assures our true safety.

CHAPTER 2
"IT DON'T COME EASY—YOU GOTTA PAY YOUR DUES" (RINGO STARR); PROGRESS

He restoreth my soul:
"...self-denial, sincerity, Christianity, and persistence alone win the prize, as they usually do in every department of life." Mary Baker Eddy in *Science and Health* (462:15–19)
"...one day is with the Lord as a thousand years, and a thousand years as one day."(II Peter 3:8)

There were certain days in the early years that I thought were pivotal. Some represented key advances because I saw people change their minds or make some pretty radical turnarounds.

From 1974 through 1980 the resistance to the idea of women military chaplains was so overt it often made you wonder if that road would ever end. From 1980 to 1985 we were also facing the recognition that there were systemic inequities that weren't yielding. Patience was a necessary virtue. We were still on the cutting edge of new advances for expanding women's roles. The changes didn't come easy, and the men weren't sure that we'd "paid our dues." Sometimes you just wanted to say, do we have to pay dues at every new unit and every new level of leadership? Some guys made a very personal investment in making sure it wouldn't be easy. Others were more subtly resistant. It really struck me that one infantry lieutenant would walk completely around a building just so he could avoid having to salute me!

Shaping new ideas takes both patience and perseverance. At times it took blood, sweat, and even, on a certain day of recognition, tears. You prayed it was all worth it and that the steps that were true advances wouldn't ever have to be repeated. The reward was that the spiritual advances were gracious and profound.

In this chapter I will follow advances and demonstrated progress, with examples of just a few of those instances that didn't come easily. However, in the end it was so comforting to know that when you felt you'd done all you could and had fought off the exhaustion, disappointment, or resistance, you could depend on your heavenly Father. It was then you found that "he restoreth my soul," and you knew you could continue on.

Honest moral courage wrestles and prevails

During the summer of 1975, I was in seminary. I trained with one of the church's active duty navy chaplains at Jacksonville Naval Air Station. He had coordinated a visit to the Mayport shipyard. The senior chaplain stood me at a position of attention in front of his desk and immediately began to berate me. He was adamant that it was ridiculous to think women could be chaplains. He sprinkled in disparaging remarks about my denomination. This went on for a long time and was only interrupted when the phone rang. That's when the junior chaplain started in. He also violently objected to women's presence in the navy and the ministry. His own church was embroiled in debating the issue of women's ordination.

The senior chaplain kept saying it was impossible to get me on a ship because the visit hadn't been coordinated. At that point I looked down to see that my biography and itinerary were visible on the top of his inbox. I reached over, picked up the papers, and said, "Could you explain why you have my biography and itinerary and it's dated almost a month ago?" He directed me to wait in the hallway.

I was initially incensed at the outright lying. I knew being angry or resentful never accomplishes anything and only adds to the decline of any situation. I went outside to think more clearly. A shipyard is a very low-lying area, and I looked down to realize my legs were covered with a thick layer of mosquitoes. As I brushed the swarms of them from my legs, blood ran down my nylons.

This jolted me into a very sincere attitude of prayer. I knew I couldn't allow a self-righteous sense of sacrifice to contaminate my thought. I truly wanted something better. A Bible passage came to me from Jesus's admonition to Saul on his journey to Damascus: "It is hard for thee to kick against the pricks." I knew I couldn't change anything, but I knew God could. This recognition turned me to the Lord's Prayer. I felt profoundly moved by the first two words, "Our Father." I realized Jesus's prayer was not "My" Father. At that moment, I clearly affirmed God was "Our Father." We did all worship the same God. I felt that this united us, and any sense of divisiveness melted away. My prayer had ceased to be just about me. Because the senior chaplain interrupted me, I never got further than those first two words. He had had a radical change of attitude. As he was leaving, he explained that he felt he needed to apologize for the way he had treated me. He informed me they could get me on a ship.

The junior chaplain had a reason for his rudeness, he said. He was very upset himself, and needed to go to the credit union for cash before he deployed. We went together. He had an impending deployment for sea duty and had been frustrated with the loan officer. I continued to read my Bible lesson and pray for us all as I waited. I was affirming that harmony was achievable here and now. Much to his surprise and contrary to everything he had been told earlier that morning, a woman met him at the door of the credit union and handed him his check. Everything had been resolved and his need was met.

At the shipyard snack bar, he began to berate my denomination specifically. He asked, "What is this stupid idea your church has of Father-Mother God?" I attempted to cite a psalm that highlighted the feminine qualities of God. He was having none of it. I knew the answer wasn't going to come by trying to convince him or by attempting to argue the point with him. I simply suggested it all boiled down to the first chapter of Genesis, verse 27. If the very "image and likeness" of God was "male and female," then Father-Mother would be the most complete understanding of God. He thought a moment and remarked he had never thought of it that way. At this point his entire tone changed. He spilled out other concerns he had about deploying on his ship. We shared many words of comfort, and again a sense of unity replaced any sense of divisiveness.

Suddenly, he got up and said it was time to go onboard the ship. We had a highly successful visit to a ship just returning to port after a long deployment at sea, after which he took me to catch my ride back home. As he left he commented, "You're going to make a very good chaplain." He drove away and then turned his car around, returning to where I was sitting on a bench. He got out of the car again to say, "No! You ARE a good chaplain."

Returning to my friends' home, I related the series of events. When I finished, the wife exclaimed excitedly, "Well, what happened to the blood on your legs?" Startled, I thought, "Oh my gosh! I forgot all about that when the supervisory chaplain interrupted me to apologize. I've been running around with blood dripping down my legs!" We all looked down expectantly, yet there wasn't any sign of mosquito bites—and the blood on my nylons had disappeared. There was a moment of hushed silence and then a "Thank you, God!"

The experience with those senior and junior chaplains was a clear example of how ready some people may be to change a belief. Those who are most aggressive may actually be showing their readiness. That may explain why they are wrestling with it in such a vocal manner. They are at least honest enough to openly object. And conversely, some who are very antagonistic may only do so behind your back. The moral courage is in the open and honest attempt to address the new idea. Moral courage is part of persistence.

My roommate and sister, Diana

The first two women accessioned into the army as chaplains were the sole women in their 1974 and 1975 Chaplain Officer Basic Courses. When I arrived at Fort Hamilton for my chaplain training in July of 1976, I found there was another woman in the class training for active duty. We became virtually inseparable and were destined to bond through the many training experiences. We were sisters of the heart for many years.

From day one in that chaplain training, the men would tell me I had two strikes against me and that I would never make it in the chaplaincy. They cited my being a woman and being of a denomination that was not looked on favorably. My roommate, Diana, was told her two strikes were being a woman and being black. We were not discouraged by these frequently offered observations. We both knew God was our shepherd and leaned on that understanding rather than the waves of human opinions. We could expect progress, which is the law of God, as Mrs. Eddy has said.

We basically ignored their predictions, and indeed my best friend Diana would be the first woman chaplain promoted to lieutenant colonel (LTC). She had an impressive career and was the first female selected to train in the area of Family Life Counseling. She retired in 1996, and we remained dear friends and sisters of the heart until her passing in 2015.

"Stand therefore, having your loins girt about with truth"
Ephesians 6:14

The Chaplain Officer Basic Course I went through in 1976 at Fort Wadsworth, New York, included a final field problem in which new officers practiced their skills in a remote field setting, including training with brand-new enlisted basic trainees. New chaplains, new recruits, and the newness of women in the military was a lot of new to put in one place. Still, I wanted to expect progress. Yet it took a while to get there.

At the confidence obstacle course, our combat arms majors, our class leaders, let me try only some of the obstacles. Even then they insisted they personally had to spot me for safety reasons. Next, the company commander I was embedded with lied to me about the start time for a road march and diverted me to the hospital to visit one of his troops. Later he drove me to the field site. That evening I went to where I had set up my pup tent and found the male cadre had pulled it up. The next thing I knew, a lieutenant and a couple of non-commissioned officers grabbed me by my feet and arms and wrestled me into the back of an RV. It might as well have been the shootout at the OK Corral, because I did not go quietly into that dark night. They drove me back to main post and rolled me out onto the lawn back at the barracks where our class advisors were billeted. I briefed our infantry major on what had occurred, and he decided he would put me with a different unit the next day.

This second company commander asked for a volunteer to demonstrate the obstacle course events. He loved the idea of a woman and a chaplain being the demonstrator. I easily did all the events. When I returned that evening, I found the chaplain instructors had informed the chaplain school commandant that I had defied their orders not to do the obstacle course. He had allegedly called the army chief of chaplains in the Pentagon and insinuated that they were considering a court-martial. This was so utterly ridiculous that I said, "Great! Let's call in the press as well. I'd love to tell them the whole story. I can see the headline now— Woman chaplain court-martialed for doing her duty." I wasn't surprised that they backed down. I was allowed to continue the training exercise, participating in all the other events.

Progress isn't always easy, and it isn't always accomplished in the ways we'd expect it to come. Progress often comes a little at a time and never seems to come as quickly or as easily as we'd like it to.

The first week is often the hardest

When I was stationed at my first regular active-duty unit at Fort Sill, I in-processed four different units during my first week and found I was rejected sight unseen by the commanders when they found out I was a woman. Our church studies a weekly Bible lesson, and that week the subject was "Love." It included some helpful and relevant passages. I prayed with two ideas from the Bible: "he is in one mind, and who can turn him? and what his soul desireth, even that he doeth" (Job 23:13), and "Who hath directed the Spirit of the Lord, or being his counsellor hath taught him?" (Isaiah 40:13).

My new artillery group commander asked me if I knew what a polar bear was. I told him I assumed he didn't mean the animal and asked if it was a weapon. He said I'd find out the next day. He told me to report to the parade field in front of the battalion headquarters he pointed to outside his window. The physical training uniform was combat boots, a white tee shirt, and green fatigue pants. It didn't include a name tag, rank, or branch insignia.

As the sun came up I realized I was the only woman among six hundred men. When the infantry commander saw me he thought someone was playing a joke on him. He told me to fall-in in the back of the formation, and he would straighten out the mistake after we finished a six-and-a-half mile run. He told me to fall out when I got tired; a sergeant always had a straggler formation. I'd worked up to running two miles in my basic course but had never run longer distances. I prayed with the Bible passage "they that wait upon the Lord shall renew their strength; they shall mount up with wings as eagles; they shall run, and not be weary; and they shall walk, and not faint" (Isaiah 40:31). I drew my strength from those passages, knowing that God would sustain me. I needed to recognize it was only for His glory. By recognizing and trusting the Bible truths, I had resources I could lean on for strength.

At about the five-mile point the commander came running to the rear of the formation. He seemed agitated and asked me if I could run to the front with him. He said there was only a mile and a half left. I nodded and ran up front with him. In the Christian Science textbook, Mrs. Eddy stated, "Whatever it is your duty to do, you can do without harm to yourself" (*Science and Health* 385:17–18). I knew it was right to do my duty and that God would help me.

Back in garrison the commander began to dress down the formation. He accused some of the soldiers of sandbagging. Usually, significant numbers of people fell out every day, and today everyone kept right on running. He said, "Just because this woman made the run, not one of you men fell out. Obviously, you didn't want to be shown up by a woman! I'll fix this. I'll run her up front with me every day." He fought to allow me to be assigned; women were not supposed to be assigned to infantry, perhaps they had never been, and he was taking a landmark step. This was recognized in the unit and beyond, as was my running with the men. This unit's organizational documents included no authorization for a chaplain on their staff, and although the other units had never wanted me before, now because of the positive publicity, they wanted me.

Everything was new territory with this assignment. When I reported to my office, it had been stripped of everything but a desk. They had never had a chaplain and hadn't prepared for one. Throughout the day other members of the battalion did come in with curtains, a file cabinet, a desk chair, etc., until the office was once again intact. But then, an enlisted chaplain assistant introduced himself by telling me he couldn't work for a woman. "My wife won't let me," he said. I told him I understood if he wanted to respect her wishes. However, he would need to explain to her what would happen if he wasn't at his appointed place of duty. For twenty-four hours he would be charged with failure to repair (report to his place of duty). Then he would be declared AWOL (absent without leave), and then if he still didn't report for duty after thirty days, he would be declared a deserter and dropped from the rolls. That meant she would eventually need to visit him in the stockade. He looked shocked and decided he could work for me.

So there was a lot of background to this situation, and gradually I came to understand it. I didn't know that the brigade chaplain, a major, had been informed of my pending assignment and was opposed to it. He refused to supervise me and passed out inaccurate and derogatory information about my denomination to everyone I'd work with. He so inflamed his supervisor, the corps chaplain, with his false facts that this corps chaplain appeared at my door just after the long run. The corps chaplain was a lieutenant colonel, which would be intimidating to the soldiers assigned at the battalion level. His rank was equal to the rank of our battalion commander, the most senior leader in our unit. Standing in the hallway of our headquarters, he pushed my door open and declared in a loud voice, "You're the devil incarnate, and you're going to Hades in a handcart and I'll be pushing it!" I turned to God and listened, never saying a word. The thought came to me to silence this lie. I felt directed to simply shut the office door in his face, and I did that. For a captain to shut the door in the face of another officer two grades higher was a huge shock. He was a veteran of over twenty years' service, and I hadn't even been in my first unit a whole day. Sometimes it takes something startling to shake loose an entrenched belief.

We needed a fresh start. I knew he would also need to know my motive was pure. I gave him a moment and then reopened the door. I grabbed both of his hands and shook them lovingly as if nothing had happened before that. I introduced myself and told the corps chaplain that he sounded upset and that perhaps we should talk. He came into my office. After showing him some direct misquotes in the articles about my denomination, he calmed noticeably. I asked him if he could respect the obvious lack of scholarly integrity in the articles. He agreed he couldn't and seemed to relax even more. I asked him if he as a Protestant chaplain believed exactly what a Catholic priest believed. He agreed no. I told him I guessed he had served with chaplains of various denominations much different than his in order to bless all our soldiers. He smiled and wholeheartedly agreed we could work together. And, just as quickly, we became dearest friends and remained so until his retirement.

My long run with the infantry was beginning to attract attention. The installation newspaper showed up the next day because a photographer from *Stars and Stripes* military newspaper asked to photograph me running with the "grunts" (infantry). Also, an Oklahoma City television reporter wanted to do a half-hour program on me. I refused to do the publicity and ended up in front of the brigade commander's desk. The colonel told me I was going to do the stories. I begged him not to force me because it would compromise my credibility with my soldiers. I told him it wasn't fair to the men who had been making that run every day for months and no one cared. We finally came to an agreement that *Stars and Stripes* could take a photo.

Next I talked the reporter into doing a story on the full unit running. She was a woman and understood what the possible backlash might be if she gave me special attention. I agreed I would talk just a little at the end if she first interviewed my infantry commander, a member of the tank company, and a member of our communications company. That would include someone from all three of the different branches that made up the 4-31st Infantry Task Force. She agreed and everyone seemed happy with the outcome.

If things hadn't been eventful enough that first week, I was informed I was required to attend a chapel meeting late on that Friday afternoon. About ten Protestant chaplains were assigned to this chapel. The senior chaplain had called us together to tell us that only four chaplains would be allowed to preach. They all came from similar church backgrounds. The only black chaplain, the only chaplain from the Philippines, and I were all told we would not be allowed to be in the preaching rotation because they knew we didn't want to preach. The two minority men didn't challenge the assumption. When I told them I did want to preach, a huge debate began.

All of the other chaplains began to argue about every aspect of preaching. Some insisted that preaching was central; others wanted to maintain a split chancel (two podiums with one reserved only for clerics to preach or speak). Next they argued about whether we would wear robes or not. Astounded at the divisive tone these arguments were taking, I simply sat in the front row watching. Suddenly, the senior chaplain realized I wasn't participating. He turned to me sitting quietly in the front pew. He demanded to know where I was on the issues.

I calmly stated it didn't matter to me whether we wore robes or whether there was a split chancel or any of the "forms" suggested. But, there was one thing I did know: as long as hatred, evil, Satan, or whatever name they chose to call it, was governing them, no one would ever hear the Word of God, no one would ever be touched by it, no one would ever be healed by it. What I thought was very important was whether people felt a profoundly powerful presence of the Holy Spirit, which would speak through us all if it found us worthy. I suggested that when they finished whatever it was they were doing up there, I just wanted to know when I was going to preach. With an edge in his voice, the chaplain said, "This Sunday!" He loudly predicted everyone would walk out.

That Sunday, the senior chaplain made a visible display of standing up in the front row and leaving as I stood up to preach. But contrary to his prediction, no one followed him. Then he stood in the back and listened. I preached that first sermon on Jesus as Savior and got rave reviews. That was pretty much the end of the overt resistance at the chapel. "The Devil" had evaporated into nothing.

I found one distinctive difference over the years between the commanders who didn't think women should be in the military and chaplains who were opposed to women being in the ministry. A commander often changed his final conclusions about your worthiness to serve if you performed at a high level of competency. Commanders were able to recognize that their pre-judgment was based on personal opinion. A chaplain was often entrenched in his resistance because he truly believed it was God who had told him you shouldn't be there. This gave an edge to the resistance, and it would last far longer than most anticipated. Only with time and the grace of God would most male chaplains accept that women were going to be allowed to serve in the chaplain corps.

The constant questioning continues—The Chinese water torture effect

As we women entered the chaplaincy, it sometimes seemed that we were starting over, often from ground zero, time after time. But time could not be a factor; God exists eternally, without moments or days. "One day is as a thousand years," and all we really need to know is His good unfolding itself.

The idea of women being chaplains was so unknown and unthinkable in those early days, I found myself constantly having to explain my very presence to people. It just didn't enter their thought. Once I was simply standing at a gasoline pump when the male attendant said, "I'm not military, but even I know you can't just waltz into the PX and buy that stuff and put it on your hat." I patiently explained I really was a chaplain.

In the commissary or PX retirees would stop and stare at your chaplain insignia. In 1982 one man at Fort Ord asked me if I was a signal officer. That baffled me. He pointed at my cross and asked me if it was a telephone pole. I explained it was the Christian cross and said I was a chaplain. He responded, "You mean a chaplain assistant." I patiently explained that assistants were enlisted soldiers. Then, I informed him that women had been commissioned as chaplains/officers since 1974. He walked away shaking his head.

Some people in the PX would tell you that you didn't fit their expectations. They'd say, "I thought you'd be big, fat, and ugly." Other times people asked me if I was "real." After about the tenth interruption to my shopping, I'd get to the point I would laugh and say, "No, I'm just a figment of your imagination!" That was easier than having to go into a detailed explanation over and over again.

The constant questioning was a bit like Chinese water torture, and all of us pioneer women in the military chaplaincy faced it to one degree or another. Some of the military women would react with anger, and like Chinese water torture, it would appear to the person who unknowingly insulted the woman chaplain that that chaplain had over-reacted. They didn't realize they might have been the tenth or twentieth person that day that had said something insulting. Or that being hit in the same place time and time again, over and over, made that place sore, then bruised, and then it just hurt. That's why I chose humor. It was a good tool to redirect these situations.

An apology from a lieutenant

In January of 1978, I was due to rotate to a new assignment. I was surprised to see in my office one of our most squared-away lieutenants, a great officer in every way. He had come because he was also due to rotate within days. He asked to shut the door and talk privately. He had a confession to make. He began to share with me that when I first got there, he thought it was funny to start little rumors about me. "I didn't really think it would hurt anyone," he confided, as I recall. "But you never know how quickly a rumor can spread and then originate a new one." It wasn't until someone else started a rumor that he and I were involved, and that got back to his wife, that he realized these idle rumors did hurt people.

He seemed genuinely repentant and asked me to forgive him. I told him I certainly would. I added that I admired him for having the moral courage to admit to my face what he had done. I remarked to him how rare it was for someone to have the wisdom to learn something from this type of experience. He left in a very humble manner.

We certainly "got around" in the rumors. I often said in the early days that a woman in the military would have to be Tina Turner, Marilyn Monroe, and ten other star-caliber women rolled into one to have done even half of what people were willing to believe about them. This type of character assassination was discouraging. At best, you hoped that your true friends and present co-workers would realize that it was unlikely anyone could be as capricious as the rumors would portray. It was very difficult to think you had any private life in those initial years. It was just one of the things that made for a very lonely feeling to your days.

Some tears are tears of joy

When the new director of chaplain personnel arrived at my first assignment in the Pentagon in 1990, I'd been in the army a little over fourteen years. I had coordinated with him on the phone earlier in my career, but had never seen him face to face. The first time I actually saw him in his office, the first words out of his mouth were, "I was so excited when I found out you'd be working for me." Very uncharacteristically I broke down in tears.

He was mortified. I'm sure he was trying to figure out how I could have possibly been offended by what he said. I was also searching my heart to identify the source of the intense emotion. Then it came to me. It was the first time in over fourteen years that anyone I worked for had welcomed me. I knew how to respond when boss after boss refused me sight unseen or attacked me verbally. I had had countless bosses tell me they had fought my assignment based on my gender. I recognized what it felt like for a supervisory chaplain to tell me he wasn't happy to work with a chaplain of my denomination. But I had never had a new boss say anything positive in the first encounter. This was foreign soil for me. It was a sign that there may have been a ray of progress for the women chaplains in the army.

Once I understood, I explained in detail the source of my shock. I reassured him that these were tears of joy. He seemed rather crushed and said he'd like to apologize for all the other men. He was a gentleman and a gentle man. I would work for him for two more years. And I can say, there wasn't even one other time he saw me cry.

Function finally trumps form

Years later, as the time came for my retirement and I reviewed the gains made by the chaplaincy and women since I had come into the service, I could not help thinking of this earlier time and one incident in particular. It had to do with uniforms. In 1979 I was invited to give the blessing for the Thanksgiving meals in several of the dining facilities of the Second Infantry Division in Korea. I needed to fly with the division commander and his sergeant major in their helicopter.

At that time the women's dress blue uniform was a poorly designed, slightly A-line skirt. I couldn't move my legs enough to get into the helicopter. Either the men had to board the bird and then pull me up by my arms, or they had to look away. I'd have to slither into the seating compartment in a very revealing and un-ladylike manner.

At one compound I lifted my leg to get into a jeep and the skirt stopped my leg movement. I nearly fell backward into the snow and slush. The driver, a private, had to put his hands on my backside to prevent me from falling. I am grateful to say he just sort of pushed me by my derrière back into the seat. He was very embarrassed, and I was mortified. That day I made a vow. I didn't care what the uniform regulations specified; I was getting pants made to my blues.

I had a Korean tailor design a pair of plain blue pants to match the jacket. I also contacted a woman chaplain in the DC area. She began to work a uniform accommodation for us. Military policewomen were just becoming gate guards at Arlington Cemetery. Women chaplains also did graveside service outdoors in freezing cold climates. We received the accommodation, and eventually the women's dress blue uniform would include standard issue two-tone blues pants like the historical cavalry soldiers wore. Finally there would be one recognizable and functional uniform for all.

When the time came in 2004 I chose to have my retirement ceremony at the Women in Military Service for America Memorial at Arlington Cemetery. Brigadier General Wilma L. Vaught, who had retired from the US Air Force, had been the spearhead for that long-overdue memorial. She asked if I would give her my uniform with the initial tailor-made blues pants for the Women's Memorial Museum. I was honored to present it to her the day I retired. She remarked that she loved the idea of a woman who knew how to get things done.

But as for me, I could "stand still and see the salvation of the Lord" as Moses said, and significant progress for women, also, when this event occurred.

In the early years as lieutenants and captains, the women chaplains faced individual resistance as well as the newness of being in the military without the benefit or protection of the authority of people with senior rank. You learned the military is a "total institution." It controls its members twenty-four hours a day. It determines what you wear, what you eat, when you sleep, and where you live. Our peers, our chaplain supervisors, and some other officers constantly predicted women chaplains would never succeed in the army. We became all too familiar with every type of individual resistance. At about the ten-year mark we would all realize that even if we made it to field grade ranks as majors or lieutenant colonels, institutional and branch management level biases still loomed on the horizon. Progress never stops making its demands upon us.

CHAPTER 3
TAKING THE FRONT RANK

. . .he leadeth me in the paths of righteousness for his name's sake.
"It is the task of the sturdy pioneer to hew the tall oak and to cut the rough granite. Future ages must declare what the pioneer has accomplished." Mary Baker Eddy (*Science and Health* VII: 23–26)

The front rank in the military is the front lines—areas of exposure to challenge and danger. The firsts in any field are worthy of note. A special sense of accomplishment can accompany a pioneer as he or she realizes this is the initial time a particular opportunity has been awarded to his or her particular group. As a woman military chaplain in the mid-1970s and 1980s, nearly any job you performed was a first. This chapter will follow just a few of the times I was assigned in areas considered to be new ground for army women in the Chaplain Corps. Yet I knew I wasn't alone in the human sense. Women throughout the armed forces were going through many challenges. We hoped as we did our duty that it might help our nation understand we simply wanted to serve. What seemed most important to me was the fact that our Father-Mother God was with us. We asked only that what we did would be to God's glory.

A moving experience: humbly beginning the Chaplain Training Program

There's always something distinctive and special about someone's "first first." When I was accepted for my church's chaplain training program, I left Iowa with one suitcase and my savings of only $250. I had no job and no place to live, and I hadn't applied for seminary at Boston University School of Theology (BUSTH). I just felt I was on the right path for my life: I wanted to be a chaplain for the Christian Science church, my own and loved denomination that had blessed my life so immensely.

When I arrived at our church headquarters, I went to the office of the supervisor for our chaplain training program. He told me to go to Boston University and inquire about entering their seminary program. I was very trusting and didn't realize that people applied several months ahead of time at a major university. I had an undergraduate degree and a year of graduate studies from the University of Iowa, but had never filled out applications before. Circumstances involving my own ability to pay and the need for a scholarship had meant I received financial aid without applying, sometimes quite literally on the spur of the moment.

I was on my own in the big city. As I walked toward Boston University, the magnitude of what I had done seemed to overwhelm me. I literally became dizzy. As I passed our church's reading room, I saw a poster in the window. It was a picture of a young girl running through a beautiful field of flowers, and it read, "Is there a substance that can't be used up?" Below the question was a Bible quote from John: "God is Love." It woke me up to the realization that God was the source of everything I needed. At that moment I knew more certainly than ever before that God's love for me would guide me.

I walked a few miles to the campus and somehow wandered into a building. I remember explaining to a man that I was from Iowa and had come there for seminary. I explained I had no money but would work for a year. I was under the impression it was too late to start this year; I was going to work to get funds for the next year. I asked if I could find out about the costs. He seemed quite moved and told me I could start seminary now. He pointed out a window and showed me which building was the seminary. Then, he wrote some notes in envelopes and told me where late registration was being held. He told me to present the envelopes to the bursar and that I would start classes in a couple of days. The envelopes must have been vouchers for my tuition because I never paid a penny of tuition myself.

I returned to our church center feeling a great sense of joy, having seen that God's love had indeed guided me. As I was waiting for the elevator, the doors opened and a woman walked out. She paused a moment and looked pensive. She told me she didn't know why she was asking me this, but did I need a place to live. I told her yes, but that I didn't know how I would pay for it. She explained that one of her roommates was getting married that weekend. Oddly the security guard at the entry point chimed in, saying, "Why don't you work security?" Because it was the 1970s, I asked him if they let women do that. He admitted he didn't know, but offered to take me to the security supervisor's office. I told the supervisor I was starting seminary and needed to work. He laughed and said, "Well, let's try it on the swing shift." By three o'clock in the afternoon, I had been admitted to seminary, I had a place to live, and I had a job.

God had certainly met my every need. I look back on that day with wonder now and recognize that moral courage yields an infinite blessing.

Reporting to the 2nd Infantry Division as the first woman chaplain

Upon arrival in Seoul, Korea, in 1979, I was told I would be assigned to the Second Infantry Division. Being the first woman chaplain to serve in a combat division, I wanted to be prepared. An inner voice urged me to immediately find out what chaplains did if there was a high level of alert. We were, after all, with occupation forces who were on constant watch for North Korean infractions. I found the more obediently I listened to that inner voice, the more I received such insights. Within hours of completing my personnel paperwork to in-process, I talked to our support operations officer (SPO). He gladly gave me the briefing I needed, which included the code word for an alert and the procedures each section was to follow if there was an actual conflict.

When I arrived at the division support command (DISCOM) chapel, the assistant brigade chaplain wanted to welcome me. We had known each other in seminary. He decided to greet me with a tray of powdered sugar donuts. Unfortunately, he tripped and spilled the donuts down the front of my uniform and on the carpet in my office. It looked as if it had snowed on the floor and me. I quickly went to the restroom and cleaned the front of my fatigues. I was on my hands and knees on the floor attempting to clean up the sprinkles of sugar when I looked up to see two sets of combat boots entering my door. Indeed, the alert whistle was going off, and it was the division commander, and his chief of staff.

The general was angry because he had sent a *Stars and Stripes* reporter to meet me at the airport. The reporter wanted to do a story on what it was like to be a woman chaplain in the division. I had told him I didn't do publicity. I recommended that as an alternative, he talk to a woman chaplain, my friend Diana, who had also just arrived that week at the I Corps Headquarters in Oiu Jon Bu. The general was angry that I had refused to do the interview because he wanted the publicity. He immediately demanded an explanation.

A passage I had studied in our denominational textbook was just the counsel I needed for this type of situation: "Speak the truth to every form of error." I discerned that I needed to be absolutely honest in this trial. I told him it seemed premature to write such an article because I hadn't even arrived at the division when the reporter approached me. I added I wouldn't think it appropriate to stand on my past laurels.

He regrouped and demanded to know why I thought I could be a woman chaplain in the division. Having been challenged in two previous assignments, I never blinked an eye. In a very respectful tone, I asked him, "What would make you think I couldn't?" He countered, "I lead the entire division on a monthly four-mile run in formation." I told him, "Great! I can kick back and take it easy. I've been running with the Fourth Battalion of the Thirty-First Infantry six to nine miles a day." He paused a moment and then threw out another challenge. "Well, we do a monthly twelve-mile road march." I countered, "Great! I can kick back and take it easy there, also. I've been doing five-, ten-, and fifteen-mile road marches with my basic trainees at the Artillery Training Center." He seemed to be rethinking some things because he realized I wasn't being intimidated.

I noticed the chief of staff was trying not to laugh and was turning his face aside. This only wound up the general a bit more. He challenged me again. "What's a Fog Rains?" I told him that was the code term for a division alert. He glanced at the chief of staff and seemed surprised. Then, I informed him I had already reviewed the plans for what the chaplain section would do in the event of an attack.

I pulled the only memorandum in my in-box. It was the general requesting suggestions from the leaders to improve procedures used in the division. I told him I had some suggestions for training. At that he broke into outright laughter. He said he wanted to give me at least a week in the division before he entertained my recommendations.

He boldly walked to my desk and dialed the DISCOM commander, who was also new that month. He told the colonel that he had been visiting work sections in the DISCOM and that there was only one place that wasn't messed up. He said, "That's your chaplain's section." That was by no means the last time I saw him. I knew there was no reason this couldn't be a harmonious transition and bless everyone involved, in the front ranks or not.

Audacious bias and fabulous schooling

Command and General Staff College (CGSC) is a prestigious mid-level military school that teaches young officers the skills necessary to serve on General Officers' staffs and is considered a sign that you are on the road to serving in the most career-enhancing jobs in the army. Army officers who are senior captains must complete CGSC to remain competitive for promotions. Each year a small percentage of officers are selected by a board of senior officers to attend a yearlong resident CGSC course at Fort Leavenworth, Kansas. In the chaplain corps only about 5 percent of all chaplains are selected to attend the resident course. The 95 percent of chaplains must complete similar course work in weekend reserve component schools at local reserve units or through correspondence courses in the evenings on their own time.

In 1984 at Fort Ord, California, the senior chaplain, a colonel, asked me to come to his office. He told me that they had received a call from the Pentagon. They wanted to inform me that I'd been selected for resident attendance at CGSC. However, the personnel director for the army chief of chaplains at the Pentagon had said they weren't going to send me. They refused to waste one of their few chaplain quotas on a woman. I was pretty shocked that they wouldn't allow me to attend simply based on their personal gender bias, because women's issues were huge at that time. I knew they didn't have the authority to nullify the results of board selection procedures that were governed by army regulations. I asked them to give me time to think about it and that I would consult a military attorney.

I drove to Berkeley, where my sister, Sandee, was in seminary at The Pacific School of Religion. When I told her about the meeting she was pretty incensed. She wanted to discuss this with her friend, the first woman federal magistrate. When Sandee told her the details, the judge wanted me to file charges, forcing a lawsuit. I told them litigation wasn't normally in accord with my religious precepts, but agreed I'd keep them posted.

My battalion commander was shocked and urged me to ask a military attorney to accompany me to the follow-up meeting with the installation chaplain. On Monday I told the installation chaplain I wanted to make sure I had understood him correctly in our previous meeting.

Amazingly, he again repeated that I had been board selected and that the branch wasn't going to waste a quota on a woman. I could see the attorney bristle when they admitted the gender discrimination.

I asked him if he understood that in essence, the chaplain branch was telling me to get out because I could never be competitive with my male peers? I can't fault them for their honesty, because they said, "Yes! That is what we're telling you." Then, the installation chaplain asked me what I'd do if I got out of the army. I told him I would want to teach ethics. I informed him that a woman federal magistrate was urging me to file a gender discrimination suit against the army chief of chaplains. Of course, this caused them great distress, and they admitted they needed to call the Pentagon again.

The personnel director at the chief's office told them to ask me if I would accept a fully funded civilian graduate degree program instead. After praying that night I was led to agree to accept the lesser civilian degree program, if they would allow me to go to Stanford University. I added the provision that they would promise to assign me to a utilization tour to teach ethics in one of the four largest combat arms service schools (infantry, armor, artillery, or air defense artillery). They agreed, probably assuming that I'd never get accepted at Stanford.

Being from Iowa, I had no clue that Stanford was such a competitive school, especially for graduate studies. I called the religious studies department and asked for an interview with the director, and he agreed. Later I realized that God had to be acting in this, because he had instantly granted me an appointment.

In the appointment I grilled the director for some time about the program. He noticed my Boston University Seminary transcripts and asked if I would be interested in Harvard. I told him no. My midwestern naiveté was more obvious than ever. I told the director that I had had an "original thought" and that is why I wanted to attend Stanford. He chuckled and told me I needed to fill out an application. I explained that I had three degrees and had never filled out an application. He assured me for Stanford I would have to fill out an application. He must have known he was dealing with a real anomaly. He did remark when I left that he could tell I really was in the military.

I was accepted at Stanford's graduate school of religion and started a master of arts degree that fall. I attended a welcome picnic for the new religious studies students that included only a small number of students and the director of the religious studies department. It prompted me to ask him if this was all of the new students. He smiled and said, "No, this is all of the doctoral and master's degree students in the entire department." I had assumed a university would have large numbers of new graduate students each year. It was dawning on me how competitive it was to get into Stanford's graduate programs. Then I asked him how many master's degree students had been admitted to the Religious Studies master's program. He pointed across the table and said, "You and that woman over there." I asked him how many people would have applied for the program. He told me that they probably couldn't count the number of applicants because there were so many. That recognition helped me realize what a unique opportunity God had given me. I was one of the first to have been awarded a degree program. I was still pushing the envelope.

Fight the good fight: My first day (and later) at the Pentagon

In 1989 I received orders for the army chief of chaplains office and was struck by the fact that my life was probably about to change significantly. I can't remember being more overwhelmed than the day I made my way into the Pentagon and realized I would be working at such an historic site with a high level of responsibility. This was truly the front ranks: exposure to challenge but also true opportunity. I asked God then and there not to ever let me misuse or misunderstand the responsibilities that would be entrusted to me.

The second day, the chaplain I was replacing trained me to prepare the files of eligible chaplains and to facilitate the voting by senior chaplains composing selection boards for competitive attendance at military schools. The board results are an order of merit list (OML) that ranks the records that received the highest votes to the lowest votes for that year's chaplain seats in all of these schools. It was one of the jobs of that office, which consisted generally of career management, and it meant that I handled the selection boards for opportunities for chaplains in their career advancement, such as Command and General Staff College, or senior service college or other opportunities. Board members voted on confidential ballots, awarding eligible chaplains a score of 1 to 6 based on the quality of their records. The chaplains receiving the highest scores from board members were awarded the school opportunity.

I soon discovered this was not going according to standard procedure.

My junior high school 8th grade (1964) photo. It was taken shortly after my healing of severe shyness.

My offical photo at the 2nd Infantry Division Support Command in Korea in 1979.

1979 at the 2nd Infantry Division Chapel, 9 miles from the DMZ. The Republic of Korea Army chaplains and the American Army chaplains pray as we received Bibles from the American Bible Society.

In the late 1980s I had the honor of re-enlisting my chaplain assistant.

Giving the invocation for the Women's History Month ceremony in the Pentagon in March of 1992 was a special treat. Elizabeth Dole (far left) was our guest speaker.

The Army Chief of Chaplains, MG Matthew Zimmerman, presented me with an impact award in 1992 for improving the accuracy of our chaplain branch schooling boards.

In October of 1998 I attended a NATO chaplains' conference in Oberamergau, a stunningly beautiful section of Germany.

As usual I was the only woman on our Army War College seminar's volleyball team at Carlisle Barracks in 1995. We won the tournamenrt.

At my promotion to LTC my husband Jeff and my best friend Chaplain (LTC) Diana James pinned on my silver Oak Leaves. Diana shared the joy of the moment with kind comments describing how we had encouraged each other from the time we were roommates in the Chaplain Basic Officer course.

In Germany in 1997 I saw my first "Frog Crossing" sign warning motorists that the roadway could be dangerously slippery. This was in spring, when frogs migrated through the area.

In 1998 I took my niece's "Flat Stanley" toy into our helicopter simulator cockpit so she could show her classmates the inner workings of flight.

In June of 1998 I was invited by the board of The First Church of Christ, Scientist in Boston to share my experiences in delivering the Easter sermon in Bosnia. The talk was delivered at the Annual Meeting of The Mother Church. The two people with me were also invited speakers.

In 1998 "Flat Stanley" also posed with me in front of the V Corps Headquarters. We are standing by one impressive tank!

One of my favorite sights in Germany was the Necar River in Heidleberg, lined with snow-crusted historical buildings.

The Koneigsee Nunary, silhouetted here against the majestic Alps, was another favorite vista in Germany.

My husband Jeffrey L. Harvey (LTC, Ret) U.S. Army, when he spoke at the Quarterly Veterans Memorial in Ocala, Florida in 2005. He served 14 years of active duty as an infantryman, including two tours in the Vietnam War and retired from the Army Reserves. He was awarded the Combat Infantry Badge, the Silver Star, two Bronze Star medals for valor and 2 Bronze Star medals for meritorious service as well as an Air Medal. He retired in 1991 and coaches and officiates football and baseball. We have been married more than twenty-four years.

In the mid 1990s The Mother Church sponsored a Christian Science Chaplains' Conference in Colorado. (Back to front, l to r) Mike Hamilton, Tom Blair, Dan Brantingham, John Babcock, and Victor Smith. In the next row down are Chaplains Ryder Stevens, Charlotte Hunter, Teri Erickson, Sandy Sandburg, and David Cornthwaite. Third row down, Chaplains Randel Croft (head above) Tom Wheatley, Dick Davenport, Bob Doughtie (endorser, Ret.) Chris Ceipley, Front Row: Chaplain Janet Horton. (Spouses and family members and speakers are interspersed in the photo.)

At my retirement ceremony, Chaplain (Col.) Donna Weddle shared how she and I worked to get a change to the Army Uniform Regulation. A new regulation gave women the latitude to wear pants with the Army Dress Blues early in the 1980s.

Personnel leadership were not following regulations; from the thousands of records, they were just pulling out people they knew and liked for selection, thus making their job easier.

My predecessor left before the week was over, and I found he had given our boss, the director of chaplain personnel, the order of merit list. I went to the director to ask about the notification procedures for selectees. Much to my shock, I found that he and the commandant of the chaplain school were rearranging names on the OML. It particularly bothered me that a minority chaplain had been moved from the top of the list to a lower position that gave him only civilian degree program eligibility. I told them that I didn't think altering the board results was ethical. The colonel pointed to his eagle insignia and told me, "That's the way it's done." I told him it seemed deceptive to give the army, the chaplain board members, and the branch chaplains the impression that selections were being made by proper procedures and then secretly to allow the "good ol' boy" network to alter the equity and equal opportunity of the merit list.

He told me, "If you don't like it, you can leave." I told him, "Yes, sir, if that's your request. But if I leave, you need to understand I will be using the second door down the hall to inform the army chief of chaplains what you're doing." He laughed and told me to do whatever I thought necessary.

I asked to see the general and he welcomed me graciously. I explained that the colonels were rearranging names on the school board order of merit list. I told him I couldn't be any part of such unethical behavior, and that I would understand if he felt he needed to replace me. However, I also told him, if that was the case, ethically, I would need to inform the Department of the Army Inspector General that such violations of procedures were occurring.

The general cringed and asked if I had the original OML. I told him I did. He instructed me to protect the documents with the official results. He informed me that the director of chaplain personnel was retiring within the month. We agreed to wait until the director went on terminal leave in about two weeks, and then I could properly administer the board results.

This first indicator became the catalyst for a much-needed and complete procedural review. As I learned the correct procedures from the Department of the Army Secretariat's Office for the promotion boards they administered, I instituted their highest standards for our lower boards governed by regulations and our own branch policy. The more I learned, the clearer it was to me what had happened behind the scenes when I was denied attendance to the Command and General Staff College in 1984.

Reviewing the eligibility zone for our school selection board, I realized that too many chaplains' files, which should have received consideration, weren't presented to the board I trained on during that first week. They did not have the complete assortment of records. One of the biggest contributors to these questionable practices was the fact that this pre-dated the use of computers. There were no databases available to professional branch offices. In order to bring equity to the system, I worked every day, including weekends, for over six months creating eligibility constructs. Being so invested in getting things right, I found I wasn't sleeping at night. I'd come home so exhausted I'd think I would surely just pass out. But my desire to figure everything out trumped the physical needs. It was only when I had manually reviewed all 1,500-plus records that I found I could sleep normally again.

Notices were published of approaching selection boards with eligibility criteria and our first review on who was in the zone. I traveled with the briefing teams and explained selection procedures and why chaplains should review their records regularly. Chaplains everywhere were appreciative, and people began to grasp the importance of understanding a career track. Our new personnel boss was joyously supportive of this new approach.

The senior leadership in the other professional branches were also involved in similar questionable procedures and inequitable practices. It wasn't long before the army deputy chief of staff for personnel (DCSPER) received complaints about questionable procedures. All the professional branches were required to brief the DCSPER general on their selection board procedures. When all was said and done, the Judge Advocate General (JAG) Corps' senior general was told to retire early, and both the attorneys and doctors lost majority membership on their future selection boards until they made corrections.

When I gave a briefing of our procedures for the chaplain corps, the inspectors said I had even higher standards than the adjutant general (AG) could provide, and our general was rewarded rather than penalized. I received an impact award and the honor of representing our office at the White House reception for Gorbachev.

I was invited to brief my JAG personnel counterparts on the new system I had put in place for our selection boards. In turn, these attorneys would help protect me in the future when gender discrimination again proved to be a challenge.

This experience taught me to make a systematic review of all my assigned areas of responsibility. I began to teach the leadership precept that officers have a responsibility to express a loyalty to the truth that supersedes the personal loyalty a commander or supervisor usually expects. It's this type of ethical commitment that kept our general from being caught off guard about a level of detail he couldn't know personally. A very senior ranking officer shouldn't need to micromanage, but he is only protected if the subordinates are faithful to the principles of equity and equal opportunity. I was grateful I chose to "Fight the good fight of faith" (I Timothy 6:12) in this early trial. This sort of front-line combat had its own rewards.

He can turn "my mourning into dancing" (Psalms 30): Front rank leadership

When you are in high-ranking leadership positions, it isn't uncommon that you become the target of ridicule, envy, or even hatred. When you walk in the front rank, you often need your spiritual armor, and it is good to be humanly intelligent in the more demanding situations.

Shortly after I arrived as the new division chaplain for the First Armored Division in Germany in 1993, a new battalion commander, a lieutenant colonel, asked me for a chaplain. I told him that the previous battalion commander had eliminated the chaplain position, but that I would be happy to help him reinstate the authorization. I explained that the chief of chaplains had a policy that he would reward any commander by filling any new authorization as soon as the paperwork entered the Pentagon. But at this time the commander had a standard number of officer authorizations, and I was sure he knew by army regulation he could choose to designate one of his captain positions as a chaplain. However, he would lose some other staff captain who was another specialty, such as a finance, logistics, or administrative officer, because his total number of officers couldn't exceed the number of slots he was given as a commander at that size of unit.

Much to my surprise, the lieutenant colonel began verbally attacking me. He told me he had no intention of giving up any of his other regular officer authorizations to obtain a chaplain. He told me he would get a chaplain without my help. I attempted to calm him and explained I couldn't recommend that the chief of staff should take a chaplain away from a commander who had paid the bill to designate one of his authorizations for a chaplain. I said I didn't consider that ethical. He became even angrier. He stomped out of my office, threatening me that I would live to regret denying him a chaplain. He had a chapel; he wanted it filled with a chaplain without designating a staff position or money to obtain one legally.

Briefing my boss, the chief of staff, on the unusual situation, I needed to explain that the army only had as many chaplains on hand as the army structure had in its unit authorizations. Budget considerations were involved. We didn't get free extra chaplains any more than the army got free pilots without budgeting and paying for the unit position for the pilot. He also had thought I could just ask for extra chaplains. I explained that because the entire army was being reduced in size that every branch, infantry, artillery, or chaplains, were also being reduced in size. At times we barely had enough chaplains to fill authorized paid-for positions. The chief nodded, understanding now, and I figured that would be it.

However, the disgruntled battalion commander then called the European command chaplain's office in Frankfurt. They reiterated the "no space" (no designated chaplain authorization), "no face" (no chaplain replacement) policy. This only revved him up to a greater extent. Many other staff officers had tales of this man's vicious and unreasonable attacks when he didn't get what he wanted. About three months into the ordeal, I realized I had a severe problem with my back. I couldn't straighten up and could only walk with great pain.

It baffled me that his harassment was clearly public and documented, and yet the leadership seemed to tolerate it because the lieutenant colonel was in a command position. I realized that I was allowing myself the luxury of feeling quite self-righteous. I'd also ignored the obvious indications that I'd begun to resent the lack of support. Needing to do some specific prayer, I turned to the Bible because it always has an example comparable to what you're experiencing. It instructs you how to look at the change of heart and thought needed to overcome such attacks.

I looked to the Beatitudes: "Blessed are they which are persecuted for righteousness' sake: for theirs is the kingdom of heaven" (Matthew 5:10). Then, I studied a Bible passage about Elisha. Creditors were hounding a widow. They wanted to take her two sons to be bondsmen. She seemed to be entertaining a similar sense of lacking something. Elisha helped her see how to meet the challenge. He queried her as to what she had in the house (II Kings 4:1–7). I realized God had given me what I needed to meet the situation. He had blessed me with wisdom and a consecrated heart to pray when I was in need of direction. Similarly, the woman told Elisha she had only a pot of oil. He instructed her that she should pour out the oil into all the vessels she could find. I understood this direction as to pour out the truth whenever I was faced with one of God's "vessels" who had been emptied of the truthful sense of the facts. I began to pray to see that the battle was the Lord's and that the lies themselves would destroy any credibility of this attack.

About four hours into my study and prayer, I realized I had spent the entire evening praying and reading my Bible and our denominational writings. Suddenly, I realized I could straighten up without pain and the back problem was healed. I was grateful that I had been able to get my self-will and self-righteousness out of the way and get in tune with God's will and His righteousness as the Truth.

The next morning I literally danced in front of my deputy's desk. I told him the Bible passage for the day was from the book of Psalms, "Thou hast turned for me my mourning into dancing." He seemed to beam when he realized I had no problem moving or even dancing.

The antagonistic commander had been going around "bad-mouthing" me in the situation. From then on I'd simply ask anyone who questioned me if this antagonistic commander had told him or her all the details of the supposed situation. I found out little pieces of information had been provided, not the whole story. Anyone taken in by his lies would always look surprised when I filled them in with the true story and say, "Well, no, he didn't tell me that." After about the third iteration of such requests on my part, they'd realize what he'd done. Soon, other commanders were experiencing his lack of integrity. He so compromised his credibility that he lost their support.

A couple of weeks later at an officer's call, a NCO was giving a class in the motor pool. The problematic commander approached me. I told him we'd talk after the class. He aggressively continued to get into my face to talk about the chaplain issue. When I moved away from him, he pursued me and began to shove me with his chest. I walked directly over to the commanding general and stood next to him. Finally, the commander backed off.

The next day the commander called. In a threatening tone, he warned me he was coming to my office. I replied that I was going to ask the chief of staff to join us for my protection and his. The chief called the commander and told him the meeting would be in his office the next morning. The commander said something on his end of the phone that caused the chief's face to turn bright red. Then I heard the chief say, "Perhaps you should remember that the commanding general personally asked me to be his chief of staff. He has you as a commander because you were on the command list." The lieutenant colonel agreed he'd be at the chief's office the next morning.

On it seemed to go

The commander again attempted to request a chaplain. The chief listened but was realistic about the lack of an authorization. The chief expected an automatic nod from me. I noted he had not given me an opportunity to speak. The chief smiled and gave me a nod. I directly challenged the commander's half-truths. I emphasized he was only hurting himself. He backed off and left.

So at this point the situation stood thusly: he wanted a "free chaplain" who was being paid for by another unit, and he had asked a Protestant chaplain to drive 104 miles across Germany to provide a Protestant service in a chapel on his local compound. It would be as audacious as an owner of an Ace Hardware store in one part of town telling a different Ace Hardware owner that he was going to take his manager and have him work in his own hardware store, but the other store owner was still going to pay the man's salary.

Immediately I received complaints from numerous Roman Catholic family members and denominational lay leaders alleging the commander had violated their constitutional right to freedom of religion, because the commander had given an order to everyone who worked under his authority that they must attend the Protestant service at his chapel on their compound. Their commander was telling his people, who depended on him for promotion and approval, that they must worship at a Protestant service. This was particularly peculiar as the commander was Catholic and should have been aware of the distress this would create.

Once again the chief had to intervene.

A new general arrived. Late in the year at the new general's leadership conference, another, also new commander attempted to stir up this issue again. He had been ill-informed by the adversarial lieutenant colonel and also told partial truths about the chaplain issues. The senior priest and I were giving a briefing on chaplain support. As Father attempted to brief, this new battalion commander attacked him. This really threw Father, so I offered to field the question.

The misinformed new commander alleged chaplain coverage was totally messed up. Still under the influence of the lies the original commander had told him, this lieutenant colonel suggested all chaplains, including the community chaplains, should be reassigned to the combat units preparing to deploy in the Balkan mission.

I introduced myself as Chaplain Horton, the First Armored Division's church lady. At this time Dana Carvey was notoriously famous for his *Saturday Night Live* character, "The Church Lady." I started by telling him that the chaplain branch was one of the three professional or "Special Branches." I followed up with, "Isn't that specccciiiiial," exactly the way Dana Carvey would say it. This broke the tension as everyone roared into laughter, saying my impression was perfect. Then I got specific. I explained that the assignments of doctors, chaplains, and attorneys were different from the usual army assignment procedures. You couldn't just send all chaplains to Bosnia. The special branches had to provide services to all combat and non-combat units as well as all the family members. There were far fewer chaplains than there were units or chapel services. That was the truth of it.

Next, I asked the new commander if chaplains controlled unit personnel authorizations. He reluctantly answered no. Then I told him I wanted to make sure I understood his follow-on recommendation, and that I wouldn't want to misrepresent him. I repeated that his recommendation to the commanding general was that all the chaplains in all our tactical division areas, to include the community chaplains, were to be sent down range with the combat task force in the Balkans. There would be no more chaplains left here in Germany, where we were. He loudly and defiantly agreed that was what he said. They should all go with the deploying troops.

I noticed he intentionally sat in the seat in front of the commanding general and his wife. At that point, I suggested he turn around and make his recommendation to the general's WIFE. He needed to assure her that no chaplains would stay with the family members. And that he didn't care if they had church services in English. And that he didn't care if a family member committed suicide, or was hospitalized and needed chaplain support. And that he didn't care about the army personnel not designated to the task force.

The further I got through the additional implications, the more embarrassed he looked. At that point the general's wife slid forward in her seat and got her face very close to the commander's. She said to him, "Yes! I'd like to hear you make that recommendation to me." Very quietly he said, "Well, I guess I didn't think that through."

After that, Father and I were then able to give our presentation in a much friendlier atmosphere. Everyone left with a better understanding of the delicacy of providing religious support to the many and varied groups who needed it with fewer chaplains than units or chapels.

The new battalion commander seemed to realize that the now infamous commander had set him up. He apologized. I don't recall anyone ever questioning the religious support plans after that. In II Samuel, "Joab saw that the front of the battle was against him before and behind." He proposed a battle array but submitted his will to God's when he recognized the battle was not truly his. He wisely affirmed, "and the Lord do that which seemeth [to] him good" (II Samuel 10:9, 12).

I do not know for certain if any woman officer had ever stood up to men in command in such a forthright way before, but I felt as if I was exploring new ground in my area. When each new step seemed like a bit of a battle, you had to remind yourself constantly that all you really wanted was to do God's will, not your own.

Promotions evoke emotions

I was promoted to lieutenant colonel in 1993, and at that time, I wasn't exactly sure where the glass ceiling was for women chaplains. I eventually became the first woman in the Army Chaplain Corps selected for promotion to full colonel. It seemed strange when this finally occurred because my best friend Diana had retired, and now I would be the senior woman chaplain in the army. Later in my career, I discovered only one other of the initial twenty-plus women chaplains in the army between 1976 and 2004 made it to the rank of colonel a few years after I did. So it truly was blazing new ground. The cloud of fire of the Children of Israel must have been going before me to illumine and designate the way.

The day the list of lieutenant colonels who were selected for the next year's promotion to full colonel was released, my boss, Chaplain (Col.) David Howard met me at the front door of the chaplain's school. He wanted to be the first person to congratulate me. I was very honored when he gave me a pair of his Eagles (colonel's insignia) to pin on during my promotion ceremony. For such a highly respected colonel to honor me this way was a show of his confidence in my leadership and performance. However, not all the men were as supportive as Dave. It troubled me when friends told me that some chaplain faculty members were not at all pleased I was promoted.

When Dave passed on unexpectedly a few weeks later, the commandant made me the director of training and told me I'd stay there to maintain continuity for a year. Later, I received a call from the army chief of chaplains himself. It was very unusual for the major general to go around the chain of command and call a soon-to-be-promoted lieutenant colonel directly. He informed me I'd be reassigned in Heidelberg, Germany, as the first woman to be a corps-level supervisory chaplain.

Then, he added that he wanted credit on his watch for assigning the first woman as a corps chaplain. I don't think he realized that my hope was that he had chosen me because I had shown the leadership and intelligence to deserve the position. I gave him the benefit of the doubt, however, that it was implied. Still, it would have been encouraging to hear the positive criteria for his choice. We women rarely had that luxury.

When I arrived at that next assignment, I also got a very explicit email from a friend detailing how unhappy some male chaplains were that I was promoted and slotted as the V Corps Chaplain. That could not dampen my joy at my new job. And I was on my way to Germany.

Intimidation doesn't work with those who bow only to God

Whenever you fly across "the pond" to anywhere in Europe, it's a pretty long haul. I'd been awake for the better part of two days when I reported to V Corps Headquarters in Heidelberg. I was told to go to the chief of staff's office immediately. The corps commander's policy was he'd have an immediate interview with all incoming officers. The chief was cordial but explained there were two awards ceremonies that morning, so the general would be officiating at the ceremonies and would see me afterward. I offered to come back, but he said, "Oh, no, you must wait for the general."

For two hours I sat in the chief's office. The general would come and sit at the table with the honorees and families but he never spoke to me. After three hours I explained I needed to use a comfort station. Much to the general's distaste that was when he finally called for me. When I returned about six minutes later, the chief told me to go across the hall to the general's outer office. The general kept me waiting another thirty minutes. By that time I was fighting back a very aggressive sense of sleep deprivation.

When the general finally called for me, he pointed at a couch. He sat in a chair that he pulled forward so we were almost knees to knees. He leaned in so his face was close to mine and began to stare into my eyes. After about two minutes, he fired off an opening volley. He said he thought chaplains were the most worthless staff officers he'd ever worked with. He continued that they were self-serving, back-stabbing, incompetent, and on and on. Then, he leaned even a bit closer and demanded, "Do you disagree with anything I said?"

I knew that it would be unwise to be pulled into his verbal trap or to appear shocked in any regard. I asked God to help me. Instantly, a thought came to me—if this man were a professional, what would this question be? It prompted me to consider exchanging the human sense of the situation for a more spiritual sense, a sort of spiritual translation process. I simply stuck to the facts as I had experienced them.

I responded, "No, general, in the first five years I was a chaplain, I had my tropical fish poisoned, I was run off the road by men in stocking masks, and I was spat on three times. However, it's another question whether that represents 2 percent of all chaplains or 98 percent of all chaplains. And if you want to know if that represents any of the chaplains in the V Corps, you're going to have to give me more than twenty-eight hours to find out."

He leaned back up in my face and once again taunted me, "What makes you think you could be a corps chaplain?" I told him I thought the army chief of chaplains saw firsthand my systems sense, leadership, and equity when I corrected the chaplain corps selection board procedures and constructed a deployment construct for Desert Storm. I paused to consider whether to add any detail to the answer and began again, "I think that Father…" The general cut me off, leaning up very close in my face for the third time and increasing his volume a bit. "You only THINK you can be a corps chaplain, you don't KNOW it!!!"

It was abundantly clear that he was determined that there would be no pleasing him. His sense of personality was a sad illusion that I wanted no part of. I held to a precept Mrs. Eddy wrote in *Science and Health*, "The Gabriel of His [God's] presence has no contests" (567:6–7). I remember thinking that I couldn't be robbed of my right to act intelligently, because I was made in God's image and likeness. I answered the third challenge by telling him that it had always been my practice to keep my mouth shut and let my performance speak for itself. He finally seemed satisfied at this point that he wasn't rattling me. Then, it was as if he flipped a switch.

I was determined that the tone could change. I asked him in a very kind and friendly tone how long he had known the Catholic Father who was our army chief of chaplains. At last, his guard and adversarial tone came down. He made a few personal remarks on their friendship and then abruptly said, "I am done with you," and waved his hand toward the door. I got up and left.

When I returned to my office, my deputy told me the general had less than sixty days left in command. I chose to focus on the fact that God was determining that my time in Europe would be productive and truly represent spiritual progress. I didn't want it to represent mere human history or reflect a selfish careerism. I wanted to strive to know God would fill this part of my career with the bounty of His goodness, and that was what mattered. I was determined not to let the general's animosity have any power in my thought. And I knew that was one thing I had control over and could make the intelligent choice not to be victimized by his power plays.

If I was a new chapter in a life that was about to turn a page, I could leave it to God to accomplish that page-turning for both of us.

The authority of a right idea

In 1985 I had begun teaching officers and NCOs the technique of analyzing the ethics of divine command morality threat mindsets. This can be summarized as utilizing certain religious beliefs (from the Abrahamic tradition) and developing them into the imperative that enemies should be "utterly destroyed," burnt to the ground. I perceived that it was vital to convey the ethical background of a rising violent streak in world politics, terrorism. Still, developing credibility in commanders' and other staff officer's minds took perseverance and thick skin. The time and its threats were a new challenge to America and the US Army, and it would take new thinking and alertness.

In 1998 the V Corps chief of staff and commander in Heidelberg, Germany, began to listen to my analysis and see its utility. The military had up to this time identified the current threats as militarily asymmetrical, that is, our forces were so superior that that would be the defining consideration in any conflict. We could always win by being better trained and prepared, and motivational, thought-based challenges were not very important. My analysis, on the other hand, was showing that the religious symbols and the power of public opinion they affected were infusing another dynamic into modern warfare. I began to call these threats asymmetrical ethical threats (AET) because the ethics that drove their actions were qualitatively different from those in our mindset. I used this term (AET) in 1998 in the religious impact analysis (RIA) I did for the V Corps commander during our planning phases prior to our Balkan missions. The Balkans were torn by sectarian strife, fighting to the death over religious and ethnic ideals.

During an exercise in Grafenwoehr, Germany, in 1998 we were set up on a multi-station video teleconference (VTC). I had a set of slides that contrasted the current mindsets. I showed how these terrorists made their decisions in the present conflicts. During my initial brief on the religious impact in the Iraq region, evaluators verbally attacked me. They demanded to know my credentials for speaking about enemy mindsets. I named my graduate degree programs, including my Stanford studies of divine command morality. They were still unconvinced. At that moment, I felt a person behind me pushing forward to get into the crowded forward portion of the briefing area. I asked him if he had something to add. He said, "Yes!" I was thinking great, maybe this guy can take some of the heat rounds I was taking in the chest. The evaluators immediately put the pressure on him. He introduced himself as a reservist from Detroit. I laughed, thinking this guy could possibly have less credibility even than a woman chaplain in these settings.

They asked him why they should listen to him. He said, "I am a native-born Iraqi. I was a company commander in Saddam Hussein's army for ten years." The briefing area became utterly silent. They asked him what he thought of my presentation. He took his fist and slammed it on the desk and said, "Chaplain Horton has hit the nail on the top of the head! And you better listen to her." Then they allowed me to finish my briefing. He would add stunning illustrations from real life in Iraq to points I made on my slides. I remember going back to my work area that night thanking God for sending a native-born Iraqi to validate my briefing!

Afterward the corps commander asked to see me privately in his military headquarters area. He admitted to me he had always thought this was a closed, cold, dark world he would never understand. But after my brief he felt like someone had turned on the lights.

Shortly after that, our commanding general was called to the Pentagon for a briefing at the chairman of the Joint Chiefs of Staff's operations center. He called me back to his work area when he returned. He mentioned that he ended up talking more about the briefing given by his chaplain (me) on the terrorist mindset than any other staff officer's contribution on the current real life situation in Iraq. He carefully avoided any "classified" detail, but told me the insights from my briefing had facilitated a decision not to strike Iraq at that time. I was grateful that God had allowed me to use my intelligence to help the military intelligence people make a more informed decision at that time. If it was going to be a new world with new challenges, I would be glad to add to our knowledge of it—and to stay right in the front ranks facing whatever came.

CHAPTER 4
PROGRESS? ONLY WITH BLEEDING FOOTSTEPS! MALE AND FEMALE

He maketh me to lie down in green pastures: he leadeth me beside the still waters.

"Earth has no repayment for the persecutions which attend a new step in Christianity; but the spiritual recompense of the persecuted is assured in the elevation of existence above mortal discord and in the gift of divine Love." (*Science and Health* 97:32–3)

As stated previously, in the earliest years, active duty women were denied the opportunity to have children. If a woman became pregnant, she was eliminated from the service. That inequity wasn't changed until the early 1980s. In the chaplain branch, the leadership originally refused to accept the idea that two chaplains could be married to each other. It was just after I came on active duty that the thought on that progressed.

Sexual harassment is as old as time. It has existed any "where" and any "when" that people and human nature existed. However, whenever public thought attempts to advance, it needs a place to present the need, and then it begins to be addressed. Only in recent times have people become more aware of the number of times women endured sexual harassment through all the millennia of the past. Over time people realized that was true for both genders. These issues remain at the forefront of thought, and there is much progress yet to be made. This issue is experienced in any large business organization, in schools, and anywhere you have people. It's not uncommon that the public looks to the military to lead the way to a more productive line of policy, enforcement, and progress in thinking about such emotional and cutting-edge issues.

In this chapter I will relate some experiences that were representative of the sexual harassment or biases faced by the female service members when I served. I have always prayed that advances would continue to be made in this very sensitive area. Considering my own private life, I can see how restrictive views about the roles of men and women and the policies surrounding those views were like shots sent to wound the dove. I came to know how to deflect these barbs of unfairness.

Engaged and unengaged

Early in 1975, I was engaged to another chaplain trainee for our church. When we informed the military office working our application packets for the chaplaincy, they asked us to come to Washington, DC, and discuss the assignments of chaplains who were married couples.

At the army chief of chaplains office there wasn't really any discussion. We were told that one of us would have to withdraw his or her application packet. The general said they would never assign two persons from our small denomination at the same military installation. They assured us in no uncertain terms that if we both submitted our packets, one would be disapproved.

Women's issues were huge in the mid-1970s, and I figured that it would be very risky for them to disapprove my application packet because it could easily become a newsworthy item. However, I knew it had been my fiancé's goal since he was very young to become a military chaplain. Neither one of us could bear the idea of the other being disapproved because of our own application. We tearfully ended the engagement. It wouldn't be until late in 1976 that a married couple would be allowed to serve in the army chaplaincy.

Putting my foot down in the face of sexual harassment

In my first unit at Fort Sill in 1976, a young captain, an artillery battery commander, showed up in the door of my office the second day. He loudly announced he had been told there was a woman chaplain in the infantry battalion that had great legs. I considered this ridiculous, as the only uniform I'd worn to work was the green fatigue pants that completely covered my legs. He demanded that I stand up. Today we would recognize this clearly as sexual harassment. That was certainly not clear from his perspective. I realized it might be helpful to change his perspective—literally.

The man was six foot eight, over a foot taller than I was. So, I rapidly pushed my chair back from my desk. I leaped with one motion onto my desktop. This put me in a position to be looking down at him. It seemed to me I needed to nip this type of public harassment in the bud if I was to have any credibility with the other men who were staff officers there in our headquarters. If the swift and graceful leap up onto my desktop didn't shock him enough, I stomped one foot and began to speak to him with authority. I needed to make it perfectly clear I was in charge of the situation. I said, "Now you listen to me! You get out of this battalion right now and don't come back until you can conduct yourself in a professional manner!"

It must have had the shock effect I was looking for because he literally ran out of our headquarters as the infantry staff cheered and applauded! There was a great sense of competitiveness between the only infantry unit and the many artillery units at Fort Sill, the US Army Artillery Center. Our personnel officer, a West Point lieutenant, walked over to me and said, "Ma'am, I think you're going to do just fine in this unit."

De-degrading the rape prevention class

In 1978 regulations required commanders to provide rape prevention training to all the women on their installations once a year. A panel of colonels made up of a commander, the provost marshal, a doctor, and a nurse were tasked to provide the instruction for Fort Sill. Their remarks were basically that women did very stupid things, and it was in some ways their fault that rapes occurred. It was probably not atypical for where thought was on the subject in that day and age. However, the longer I listened to the speakers blaming women, the more uncomfortable I became, until I couldn't hold my tongue any longer.

I stood and asked if I could make some remarks. I told them that I thought their perspectives on the violent crime were insulting to the integrity of women. I volunteered that these crimes were far more complex than what was being taught in the class. I pointed out to them that a number of men in the infantry battalion where I was assigned had been raped. One first sergeant was so ignorant of the crime that he had laughed and told the man he should have laid back and enjoyed it. The soldier realized that the "top" sergeant didn't even comprehend he had been assaulted by a civilian man. They said nothing. I told them that I wasn't going to stay unless there was a more informed manner of addressing rape prevention. I got up and left, and all the women followed me out. Many thanked me for my comments.

The next day I was summoned to the commanding general's office. He and I were once again discussing a situation out of the ordinary. I told him that I could teach a better class than what had been presented. He said "Fine! That's just what you're going to be tasked to do."

My chaplain assistant and I put together a class that was well received by women and men. When I served at the army chaplain school, I attended the New Jersey State Police Academy's sex crimes investigation and analysis training. Over my twenty-eight years in the service, I would expand that instruction. I worked with the military police when children were assaulted in the Fort Ord area, as well as counseling convicted offenders in the stockade. I often felt I had uniquely seen this challenge from nearly every possible perspective. This included assisting law enforcement responders, duty personnel at the crime scene, and the children and adults who were victims from the moment of reporting through their recovery. I also learned that many convicted offenders had repeatedly experienced sexual and physical abuse early in their lives.

Over time I gained the most profound insights on helping when I worked with children who had those types of experiences, and found that the same insights were strikingly helpful to adults. I developed classes for units, classes for military police responding to the rape scene, and standing operating procedures and checklists for duty personnel involved in reporting the crime.

In the late 1990s some medical personnel submitted my lesson plans to the Department of Defense (DoD). I became aware of that fact only when one of the nurses called me and told me the DoD had adopted my materials. This was just one other area in which the progress couldn't come nearly as quickly as you prayed it would. However, every step of progress in this very delicate issue blessed every victim, their families, and our society as we grew to understand more compassionate and helpful ways of responding.

The third time may constitute a pattern

When you have a long-term relationship with a unit, you may find some patterns emerge. The commander begins to look to the chaplain as someone who has a pulse on the leadership climate. My rule of thumb became that one complaint constitutes an isolated case, two means you need to monitor the issue closely, and the third may indicate a pattern or problem person. I became concerned the third time I heard a counselee complain about a high-ranking NCO who was giving preferential treatment to enlisted women who would sleep with him. Conversely, he was penalizing those who wouldn't. I began to investigate the trend and found other women confirmed the allegations but were reluctant to make a written complaint. This only worked to enable the possibility of such behavior by the first sergeant. The heart of the problem was the fear of retaliation. Many believed reporting the harassment would end their careers.

When there weren't formal complaints to charge the man, I briefed the battalion commander on the trend of allegations by credible soldiers. He sincerely wanted to do the right thing. I also outlined for the commander what I thought might at least stop the behavior. He gave me the "go ahead," and we agreed to monitor what happened once I talked to the NCO.

I went to the first sergeant's office and told him that I understood that being in a very visible position of responsibility could possibly set you up as a target. Then I admitted that I couldn't discount the number of soldiers who had alleged he had made inappropriate sexual advances and abused his authority. I assured him, if it weren't true, I would be the first to make sure he wasn't the target of a set-up by a disgruntled group. I would work, in that case, to protect his rights. But I also needed him to understand that I would be just as committed to support my soldiers if the allegations against him could be proven. I informed him the entire chain of command was committed to do everything within their power to make sure he would be prosecuted to the fullest extent.

Then I explained to him I was going to speak to him as his chaplain. I told him I personally believed that dishonesty and acting harmfully towards others were destructive behaviors. I told him, in my experience, offenders didn't need any outside influence to destroy them because they were usually too busy destroying themselves. I told him it was now up to him which way it would go. He thanked me, and I left feeling more strongly than ever that the allegations were true.

In the early 1980s it was difficult to protect a whistle-blower. In that atmosphere, I was at least encouraged to know we had indeed stopped this individual. Many of the women were shocked when he actually ceased his inappropriate behavior.

Riding the Metro in DC under the watchful eyes of my brothers in arms

If I rode the Metro in DC in uniform during the time I was at the Pentagon the first time, in 1989, it inevitably evoked non-stop, repetitive questions from other commuters or requests to provide counseling. Some commuters saw the cross on my collar and attempted to impose their religious beliefs or argued that women shouldn't be in the ministry or the military or both. I found a bit more privacy if I traveled in civilian clothes. Even that was not foolproof.

One day, coming home from the Pentagon, I was quietly reading. A man who sat beside me asked me out. I thanked him and told him no. He continued so aggressively that I moved to the next car back when the train made its next stop. He followed me. Then I noticed some marines saw him follow me to the rear car. They also came to the rear car. When he continued to harass me, I moved to a different seat. At this point the marines surrounded me and told the young man to get off the car at the next station and wait for the next train. The man didn't fuss with them. I thanked them, and they gave me an "Oouh Rah" and declared in that proud marine way, "We take care of our own." I'll always remember their kind concern for me. I've often thought there were times when it would be good to have your own marine escort to ride larger subway systems.

The Pepsi-Cola baptism

After a hot, humid tennis match in Manassas, Virginia, I stopped to get a soda. I had the top down on my convertible and started through a green light. I suddenly realized a Cadillac to my right was running the red light. I slammed on my brakes. The driver was laughing about the near miss and made a lewd gesture. Then he proceeded to speed up or slow down to block the on ramp to Interstate 66. My doubles partner, a federal agent, was seeing the whole thing from her car behind me. I slowed to a crawl and he raced up the entrance ramp. My friend and I were barely able to enter the ramp in time.

When I merged onto the interstate, the Cadillac slowed down and came uncomfortably close to my car. Several times he came within inches of my car. The last time I couldn't believe he missed me. This seemed particularly odd because you could see that his new car still had the price sticker on the back window. He seemed determined to harass me, as he continually made very lewd motions with his hands and mouth. If I slowed, he slowed. If I sped up, he sped up. No other vehicles than my friend's were within visual contact. In those days cell phones hadn't been developed. I remember thinking I needed to call on God.

As I prayed, he again veered toward my vehicle. My thought went to my huge glass of Pepsi. He was dangerously close to my passenger side door, and the intuition came to me to wake him up. I tossed the entire Pepsi into his window. It sprayed in all directions. He braked immediately and pulled off the road. Then I was able to drive quickly to the next exit and take a route back home on well-populated secondary roads.

I kept wrestling with what I had done. I couldn't put the whole thing into any kind of understandable context. I asked God to help me regain any kind of productive perspective on it. When I got home, my friend called. She thought he was obviously intent on a malicious purpose. All of a sudden, it occurred to me that a little interior car cleaning on his part might be a far lower toll to pay than a serious car collision.

As a federal agent, my friend said she was sure he was under the influence of whatever spirits he'd imbibed. Although I'm quite certain the Holy Spirit had nothing to do with it when I tossed my drink at him, he symbolically got a Pepsi-Cola baptism. That would undoubtedly be the most unusual baptism I'd ever perform during my twenty-eight years as a military chaplain. It was a relief to realize no one was hurt in the process of learning not to sexually harass other drivers or to drive while impaired.

Chaplain Dearie, Cutie or Barbie—Harassment of women in the Pentagon

Being a woman in a largely male-dominated environment was often challenging. However, in rare moments your male counterparts would defuse the abuse and show support for women in the military (me) with humor and affirmation. In the early 1990s, when I was still at the Pentagon for the first time, I had several incidents that would probably be representative of the various levels of sexual harassment that women experience.

One day after a run, I was entering the Pentagon at corridor eight. I got to the door just ahead of a navy captain. Because I was in my military uniform, I appropriately held the door open for him. That particular entrance is unusually busy. People were piling up behind the man because he stubbornly refused to go through the door. I reminded him that I was junior to him and explained that was why I had opened the door for him. He barked at me, "Listen, dearie, just go through the door!" His tone of voice was condescending, and he made the remark in his loud command voice. I felt I needed to correct this very public indiscretion. I reminded him that in uniform he could address me as chaplain, or major, or even ma'am, but that he couldn't address me as "dearie." Large numbers of the officers in the entrance applauded in recognition of the correction. He became so irate he refused to enter. He stomped off in the other direction to the athletic club. Our priest and a Protestant chaplain who were with me remarked how inappropriate the man's address was at work.

We all proceeded to the snack bar inside the Pentagon to get a drink to ease our thirst. As I was attempting to pay for my drink, the young male cashier also made a suggestive remark. He called me "baby doll" as he took my money. I could hear my two friends behind me laughing. We continued into the corridor that leads to the army chief of chaplains office and passed some contractors painting the walls. As I walked by they called me "cutie" and made a remark about my long legs.

I was amazed because three remarks in the space of a few minutes was a record for me. I asked my chaplain buddies if anything unusual had happened when they entered the Pentagon that morning. They asked what I meant. I asked them if someone was giving all the men testosterone shots at the door. Of course, they thought that was hysterical. Little did I know that remark number four was just around the corner. A civilian worker approached and asked me if I had been the model for the new Air Force Barbie Doll. By this time the guys I worked with were beyond amused. I said "No!" and explained that the green uniform I wore indicated I was army. That one truly baffled me.

The next week I had a school selection board. When I put on the jacket to my green uniform, my nametag caught my eye. The guys had replaced my normal nametag with one that read "Dearie." I yelled out to the surrounding cubicles, "Okay, guys, where's my real nametag?" You could tell they were all acting very busy, and no one would admit to having done the deed. Fortunately, I had another nametag in my desk drawer.

Sometime later I found an article on my desk. A women's liberation group had broken into a toy factory and exchanged all the voice boxes in the new Barbie dolls with the voice boxes from the new GI Joe dolls. The GI Joes now said, "Let's go shopping!" and the Barbie Dolls said, "Make my day!"

Unfortunately, not all of the incidents were light-hearted. Some were quite disturbing. I remember walking down the hallway when I felt a man come up behind me. He leaned over my shoulder and placed his cheek on my cheek. He made a suggestive comment and grinned. I asked him if he wanted to remain a lieutenant colonel. He looked very shocked, and his lewd grin disappeared. He hustled off, craning his neck in all directions to see if anyone had seen what he'd done.

Another afternoon I changed into my tennis clothes. Our computer technician and I were heading to the tennis courts at Fort Myer. As I walked out the door someone motioned him over to a cubicle. I didn't realize he was no longer right behind me. A reserve component officer, who was only days from retirement, came out of his office and grabbed me around the waist. He pushed me up against the wall and attempted to touch me inappropriately. Remembering my gymnast training in college, I was able to shove him away. I told him that I would press charges if he ever touched me again. He fled down the hallway.

I realized another officer had touched me inappropriately. This occurred in the time just before he was changing stations during my California tour. We women realized you really had to watch guys right before they were leaving. We theorized they figured time was short, which made it very hard to process charges or to be disciplined. We called it the "pat on the back side as the guy went out the door" syndrome.

Through the years I would hear of similar experiences from other female officers and enlisted women. Sexual harassment is an issue that women in all walks of life wrestle with. It is increasingly harder for people to get away with severe and repeated acts of harassment in the twenty-first century age of technology, but it isn't a problem that has disappeared.

This problem was not a problem unique within the military by any means. The incident reminded me that my sister had told me a man in an elevator once grabbed her breasts before exiting on his floor. Her civilian corporate environment was no less vulnerable to individual actors who were unethical in this regard. That insight about these types of experiences was essential to understanding the pervasiveness of the issue. I believe what was key in my recognition was that these types of actors only represented a small percentage of the military or civilian community. I would pray that even those small numbers would decrease as mankind advanced to cherish the spiritual purity of all God's children, both female and male, and that not one woman or man would have to wrestle with the sense of having been aggressively touched without their consent.

A whale of a time at the Virginia Military Institute (VMI)

A friend teaching in the ROTC department at VMI invited me to their football game about 1989 or 90. The US military academies had integrated women in 1974. Institutions like VMI or the Citadel were already over fifteen years behind most other academies in acknowledging women's rights or the value of their contributions in the military. Legislation was being considered that would withdraw government funding from any schools that didn't admit both genders.

At the game, a group of men climbing the bleachers were wearing tee shirts that said, "Save the males" and something to the effect of "Keep women out of VMI." They were aggressively vocal and had obviously been drinking heavily. They sat down directly behind the ROTC department cadre and me.

One of the guys directly behind me poked me in the arm a couple of times and repeated loudly, "I bet you think women should be allowed to attend VMI!" I ignored him. The third time he was more aggressive and leaned down in my face. I could smell the strong odor of alcohol on his breath. I realized the gravity of the situation had just cranked up a notch. I spoke to him in authoritative yet measured tones. I told him I did not believe women should attend VMI and turned away. I really thought that would stop the harassment.

However, he was not going to be denied a debate. He yanked my sleeve and demanded to know why not. I figured it was time to end the physical and psychological bullying. I told him intelligent women would choose highly ranked colleges and universities or would attend an official U.S. military academy. He demanded to know what college I had attended. I began to tell him that I had four degrees and had attended schools in Iowa, but before I could finish, he interrupted with a laugh and made a disparaging remark, saying, "Is that all?"

Because they had drawn the attention of many of the people around us, I continued telling him I also had graduate degrees from Boston

University and Stanford University. I asked him if he knew anything about Stanford. He didn't respond. So I told him it was one of the most highly ranked universities in the United States, that some of the military officers in my ROTC department at Stanford worked on the particle accelerator, that it was also home to the Hoover Institute. I concluded with the fact that Admiral Stockdale had been there when I was a student.

I continued that in sports Stanford had the Elways and John McEnroe and other world-class athletes, that women like me had much higher standards and would never settle for some minor academy that had ranked absolutely last in the latest ROTC rankings. Winding up, I stated emphatically that I worked in the Pentagon, and women like me had no desire to teach at or attend an institution lost in the past and out of touch with the future and advanced ideas. That seemed entertaining to many of the fellow spectators, who laughed loudly when the drunken men seemed at a loss for any come back.

At that point the drunken men stood up. My fellow army officers had had about all they were going to tolerate. The ROTC instructors on both sides of me stood up. They were both well over six foot four. Security came quickly and removed the drunken students from the bleachers. That ended the debate that day. VMI would integrate women, but not until 1997, nearly twenty-three years behind the U.S. military academies.

Stand by me! Was that asking too much?

In 1991 I met my husband-to-be Jeff. He was a reserve officer, and he was teaching the reserve school in Dover, Delaware. He was teaching Soviet tactics and I was in his class. He asked "Who knows the nine principles of war?" and could not conceive of the fact that a woman chaplain would know the nine principles of war. I did. After a few more military history questions, he was impressed with me. I was not impressed with him and wrote up a searing evaluation of him, even though, as a friend said, "He is so cute." My friend believed he was flirting with me and apparently it was true.

He retired about that time and asked me out; we began dating and I found that this widower was truly kind and admirable. My snap judgment had been wrong. The relationship evolved into a marriage.

We had told all our friends we would love for them to join us at our new home in Annapolis. We both distributed invitations to all our co-workers that encouraged our friends to grace us with their presence but there was no need to bring a present. On that special day not one of my chaplain co-workers from the army chief of chaplains office in the Pentagon attended our wedding. This was striking to all our other guests, who repeatedly asked why no other military chaplains I worked with were present. Neither Jeff nor I could think of any answer, and it troubled us both that we couldn't conceive of one.

I had hosted some of the chaplains in my home for lunch and Naval Academy football games. I had cooked everyone in my office any cake or pie of their choosing on their birthdays. I had often attended hails and farewells at their homes and nearly any other type of social event the office celebrated. It made no sense to me.

In sharp contrast, every single person from the First Army operations center where Jeff worked attended our wedding. Even the duty person that day called and congratulated us and insisted on sending us a present. Jeff didn't attend another chaplain function until my farewell from that Pentagon tour.

That was by no means the only time I felt the isolation, and it wouldn't be the last. It did help prepare me for what would occur at my retirement ceremony.

All my many children (Dedicated to Ryan, Heather, Gretchen, Rachael, Nathan, Tony, Ivy, Michelle, David and Bridgette)
One Friday afternoon shortly after entering the chaplain training program in 1976, my church supervisor called me into his office. He asked me what I thought about the Department of Defense policy that didn't allow women to have children and remain on active duty. I told him I still needed to pray about it some more.

I have never thought of humans as Creators. I knew one heavenly Father-Mother God created us all. Children may come through us, but we, as humans, are not Creators. It came to my thought that I should read some hymns. One hymn in the Christian Science Hymnal stood out to me. "O Love, our Mother, ever near, To Thee we turn from doubt and fear! In perfect peace our thoughts abide; Our hearts now in this truth confide: Man is the child of God" (CS Hymnal # 232). I felt a distinct sense of peace that God was in charge of being the Father-Mother of the universe. It came to me with a great sense of joy that I'd have thousands of children—and most of them would be army green.

Over the years my husband Jeff and I would parent young enlisted junior officers and chaplains that we knew. It was uncanny how many times they would coin the name "Mom" for me. I have been blessed a hundred-fold in that category. What they've given me is beyond measure. I thank God that He let me be even the smallest part of their lives. The psalmist David said it best in Psalm 68:6, "God setteth the solitary in families."

The concepts of male and female can be purified and elevated. I saw that in my own experience.

CHAPTER 5
TO "KNOW EVEN AS ALSO I AM KNOWN"
. . . thou anointest my head with oil;
"...now we see through a glass, darkly; but then face to face: now I know in part; but then shall I know even as also I am known."
(I Corinthians 13:12)
You, not what you think you think you see, You, you are the best of me.   Soulshine Album, by Jay and Tessa Frost

The number-one lesson I learned in Sunday School and all through my religious studies was to see the good in others, even if they themselves weren't seeing it at the time. I was always struck by how many times healing followed a more spiritual sense of who a person was as a child of divine Love, the Creator of us all. Jesus was the master of this type of seeing. I had to begin by being as kind to myself as God is when he looks at his little ones. I struggled so much with seeing myself as worthy or good when I was young that I had to get that right before I could be of any help to others. That's when I got my first glimpse of how I was known by God. I think we all yearn to be seen for the best in us. The following experiences showed me the many ways seeing oneself and others as God's children brought healing or comfort not only to me but to others once I had grasped the concept myself. This chapter is about seeing as God sees.

Knowing who you are and whose you are
When my family moved to Oklahoma, my dad simply took my brother and me to our new school and dropped us off. Because I was a small girl, the size of a second grader, I couldn't convince the principal that my younger brother and I weren't twins. Later that morning a secretary reviewed my file and took me to the sixth-grade room. At recess I played

with another quiet young girl. I had no concept of race, nor had I ever seen persons of color. By the second recess the white children cornered me against a brick wall. A girl who was probably well over five feet tall stepped out in front and demanded to know, "Are you a Yankee, or are you a Rebel?"

Even at eleven years old, I knew who I truly was, and that it had nothing to do with what state I lived in. What I did know was that it had everything to do with the state of a person's heart. I knew from Sunday School that included loving my neighbor, but it didn't include any man-made, artificial divisions. I knew with certainty and precision "who" I was and "whose" I was. I remember saying with more authority than I'd ever spoken with before, "I'm a Christian Scientist."

The children hadn't anticipated a spiritual answer. The young girl looked to the other children, who just looked very puzzled. Then she simply said, "Well, OK, as long as you're not a Yankee." The children had no criticism for an answer that was based on my Christian identity. The situation melted naturally into one of acceptance.

The world doesn't have to be divided into contentious factions if we're all God's children.

Seeing shyness for what it really is

When I was twelve years old, I heard a fellow student refer to me as "that really smart girl!" He laughed and said, "Girls who are walking encyclopedias should remember—reference books are never taken out."

I cried that night. After realizing that feeling sorry for myself accomplished nothing, I began to pray about the situation. I realized I needed to make an effort to understand God better. I decided for six months I would read at least one page in Psalms or Isaiah and a page of a chapter in the church textbook called "Footsteps of Truth." As I prayed about the shyness, I received a much-needed rebuke. I heard a voice say very firmly and very pointedly, "This is nothing more than selfishness!" That led to an important awakening on my part. I realized if I thought people were looking at me all the time and critically evaluating my modest dress, etc., then I did think I was the center of attention.

Then I read a Bible passage: "The Lord God hath given me the tongue of the learned, that I should know how to speak a word in season to him that is weary" (Isaiah 50:4). It turned on a light for me, and I realized I didn't need to be embarrassed about being intelligent. God had given me the intelligence for a purpose, and I knew it would have something to do with comforting people in need.

By the end of the school term, I had gone from being the shy, invisible girl to being vice president of my class, president of the choir, class student council representative, and a cheerleader. I realized that a transformation of thought had transformed my experience. I think of that radical change when I read Psalm 94, "Unless the Lord had been my help, my soul had almost dwelt in silence."

The person you think you see or a child of God?
While in college in 1972, I needed to contact a bluegrass band for a house function. A friend pointed out the bandleader in the student union just as his friend unintentionally cut the man's finger with a knife.

I quickly approached them and asked his permission to help stop the bleeding. He said, "Sure!" As I held his hand in mine, I repeated Ezekiel 16:6, "And when I passed by thee, and saw thee polluted in thine own blood, I said unto thee when thou wast in thy blood, Live; yea, I said unto thee when thou wast in thy blood, Live." The bleeding stopped immediately, and he just kept looking at his hand. He gladly agreed to provide the music for our dance.

The night of the dance, he kept asking what I had done to him. I assured him he was a child of God. I told him God wasn't bound by limitations. I cited examples from the Bible where Jesus constantly defied material laws. He walked on the water, healed withered limbs, changed water to wine, etc.

Two weeks later, rather late in the evening, he demanded I go off campus with him to the house where he lived. I listened and felt God assuring me this was an exceptional case and I should go. At his house he covered a kitchen table with drugs from many ingenious hiding places within the floors and walls. Then he tore open and flushed thousands and thousands of dollars of drugs down the toilet, declaring that after I had stopped the bleeding on his hand he couldn't sell them anymore.

Again he demanded to know what I had done to him. It came to me to ask him if he could promise to answer one question honestly. He agreed, and I asked him if he wanted to be free of this activity. He paused and then quietly said, "Yes! But there's no way you could have known that." I explained that one form of prayer was a deep and sincere desire. I told him God knows what's on a man's heart. He obviously had wanted to be free of this immoral activity. He admitted that when he heard the Ezekiel passage he felt God was telling him he had wasted his life.

When I returned to my dorm that night, all the women asked me if I was the stupidest person on earth. They remarked that everyone knew he was the biggest drug dealer on campus. I told them that I had never seen him as a drug dealer. I agreed that he himself had become confused and thought he was a drug dealer. It was only when he began to realize he wasn't truly a drug dealer that God sent the help he needed. God could only send someone who knew he wasn't really a drug dealer to help him. Once I met him, I realized he was a guy I had seen formerly with his dog on campus. No matter where he was, you saw Missy, and I just hadn't remembered the connection. I had seen the tenderness in the way he talked to her back then. I saw the distinguishable gleam of his spiritual individuality. Even if he had completely lost sight of the fact he was a child of God, I couldn't have helped him if I had.

Now he moved out of the house. We were able to find him student employment. Two years later, he called me to say he was living out west and had joined a church. He shared with me that one recent day his fellow brick masons had taunted him because he no longer cussed, smoked, or drank. A few moments after the taunting, that dog of his, Missy, chased a semi at the construction site and was crushed by one of the wheels. The men again heckled him: "If you're saying you're a Christian Scientist, then heal your dog." He picked her up and prayed. He turned to God with all his heart and all his soul. He gave her back to her Creator in his heart. Within a few moments she jumped up, completely healed. He explained he wanted me to know how grateful he was to God that he had the opportunity to pray to save her life, as he always credited her with having saved his.

From that time forward, I found the women in my dorm nicknamed me chaplain even though I was our house's senator in the student government. I had no idea I would eventually become a military chaplain. Even more telling was the fact that he was a Vietnam veteran. It didn't occur to me how fitting that was until I retired and looked back on the events that brought me to that unexpected turn in my life.

A new chaplain assistant and a radically new view of a woman

In Korea in 1979, I got a call from the division chaplain's office telling me I'd be getting a new private. They warned me that they thought she was mentally retarded and I would probably have to put her out of the army. I remember thinking that I didn't want to automatically write anyone off. I'd never want to underestimate the power of prayer and God's infinite possibilities for all his children. My whole team agreed that we would embrace the woman with a warm welcome when she arrived. We worked to commit ourselves to the idea that we could discern her value and spiritual identity.

What we actually found was she had never been socialized. She had never been taught how to take care of even her simplest human needs. We taught her how to brush her teeth and cleanliness practices. I had an amazingly talented NCO who made tapes of her speech and sent them to be analyzed by therapists in Hawaii. They sent us tapes of exercises to help her work on a speech impediment. All of us began to systematically teach her about the military. We each devoted time every day to teaching her something new. But most importantly, we invested in making her understand that she was a cherished team member.

The woman underwent a transformation that the unit ministry team at the division chaplain's office labeled as truly amazing. When I left Korea about six months later, she was teaching the filing class for clerks new to the division. She was gaining confidence, and we firmly established she indeed was not retarded. She called me about a year later to let me know she'd been promoted to specialist. It was a team effort that enabled her to continue to grow in grace. In our denomination we sometimes call that "perceiving our spiritual identity."

Communications? Motivation? or Leadership?

At the US Army Chaplain School, I was teaching a communications module for the Chaplain Officer Basic Course. I decided to combine the instruction for our new chaplains and a new enlisted chaplain assistant class. I wanted to illustrate certain things about communication between officers and enlisted service members.

I positioned one chaplain and a chaplain assistant almost knees to knees on the platform at the front of the classroom. I asked the private to tell his chaplain, in his own words, what he thought his new job would be. I chose the young man because he was enthusiastic and seemed very excited about his service. He assured the chaplain he would pre-screen all counselees and make sure the chapel was set up for services correctly, regardless of whether the service was Catholic, Protestant, or Jewish. He told him that he'd recommend that any soldiers he knew with problems should talk to the chaplain. He bubbled over with enthusiasm about working in the chapel.

At that point, much to the shock and horror of the entire cadre in the room, the new chaplain leaned forward in his chair. He got up uncomfortably close to the private's face and in an almost threatening tone said, "That's NOT what your job is!" He went through a litany of scrubbing dirty tile floors on one's hands and knees, setting up the chaplain tent in the field, pulling all the maintenance on the jeep. He leaned even closer and said, "Son, I'm a noncombatant, and you better get out on the range and become a sharp shooter. Your most important job is to provide security for me on the battlefield."

The classroom was so quiet you could hear a pin drop. You could just see that the young private's positive demeanor had completely wilted. The chaplain had finished with a smug, self-satisfied look on his face and leaned back in his chair. After a thoughtful and almost painful moment the assistant seemed to revive. He leaned forward quite close to the chaplain's face and he barked out a loud, "Yes, sir, that is very important!" And then in a matter-of-fact tone he added, "And sir, your job is—to make me want to." The entire classroom erupted in gales of laughter.

I quickly intervened. I sent them both to their seats. I cracked a bit of a smile and announced that, contrary to the class syllabus, today's class wasn't on communication; however, it was an exceptional class on motivation and leadership. Almost everyone left laughing except for the chaplain in the exercise.

A call to a higher authority

In my first Pentagon tour, 1989–1993, I worked with a marvelous technician. She had recently had her third child during Hurricane Andrew. A few weeks later, I got a tearful call from her explaining her car had been stolen. When she and her husband had attempted to report it to the DC police, the desk officer assured her they never recovered stolen vehicles. Either the cars disappeared in chop shops or they would find them completely trashed. They recommended she should just call her insurance company.

She asked me to pray with her about the situation. I suggested we start by recognizing that God never made a thief. The Bible assures us

He made man in his "image and likeness." I proposed that just because some people may have become tragically confused enough to consider themselves a thief, we didn't need to be any part of making them thieves in our hearts. Then I asked her if she believed that for all times Christ Jesus was a Full Service Savior. I recalled that the prophet Jeremiah had affirmed "there is nothing too hard for thee [God]" (Jeremiah 32:17). She agreed with great joy and calmed noticeably. I affirmed Christ Jesus was our Savior from fear or any sense of loss.

I suggested it would be most effective if we prayed from a standpoint of spiritual strength. We began to be grateful for her husband's motive for getting her the newer car. He'd done so out of love and concern for the safety of their new baby, Andrew. I told her we were going to affirm that God is the source of all our blessings. I've always loved the passage from Ecclesiastes 3:14, "I know that, whatsoever God doeth, it shall be forever: nothing can be put to it, nor any thing taken from it." We agreed that what God gives us couldn't be taken from us. She told me she was going to invite her church's prayer group to join with us in prayer.

That Saturday morning I was reading my weekly Bible lesson, and a passage really struck me. Mrs. Eddy stated, "Jesus demonstrated the inability of corporeality, as well as the infinite ability of Spirit, thus helping erring human sense to flee from its own convictions and seek safety in divine Science" (*Science and Health* 494:15–19). To me it was affirming the greatness of God and that His infinite abilities are not limited to man's ways. It spoke to me as a reminder that we all need to know the best place to seek safety is in the assurance that God, as omnipresent Love, governs the universe. That establishes the fact that He can do anything. He is the true source of all the good we receive.

As I thought about the passage, it came to me to look at the clock. I made a mental note of the exact time. Then I saw in my thought a vivid picture of two men fleeing away from a vehicle. I didn't know it, but at that very same time a DC police cruiser noticed a car it thought was stalled on the side of a street. The police cruiser had to go to the next intersection to turn around in order to enter the opposite side of the roadway. As the police report noted, when it approached the vehicle, two men were seen "fleeing" from the car.

My technician received a call late that afternoon that the police had recovered her car. Much to the shock of the police and everyone who heard about it, her husband's expensive construction tools were all still in the trunk. Their claimed dry cleaning was neatly on the back seat. The car was unharmed, and the only problem seemed to be that it was out of gas.

As best the police could reconstruct the events, they theorized the men had become confused when the car ran out of gas. They had the hood open and appeared to be trying to restart the car when the police arrived, attempting to help them. Because the car was in perfect shape, it was only when the men ran away that the police realized it was a stolen car. Andrea and I couldn't stop rejoicing in how amazing God's grace was. To have the car back, intact, in less than three days was truly a wonder. It is always powerful when people join together in prayer and realize that evil ways have no power to dictate what a man, woman, or situation is.

An uncommon approach to a very common duty for chaplains

In 1997 in an operations briefing in Heidelberg, Germany, for the V Corps commander's change of command ceremony, the invocation was the first item discussed. I was seated in the back of a large meeting area. The general was asked if he had any directions for the chaplain. He merely shouted the words "short! Short! SHORT!!," progressively becoming louder with each repetition.

Because of his adversarial tone in our original meeting, I wanted to open my thought to the fact that there can always be a harmonious resolution for any situation. This line from a hymn popped into my head: "Love is not the author, of discord, pain and fear" (Christian Science Hymnal Hymn # 374). I was aware that the prayer would be given in an extremely large public ceremony. I tried to affirm that the general had every good intention for wanting it to be short. But I felt it needed to be very good because so many people would hear it. At just that moment a thought from our Christian Science textbook came to me: "[God, the divine] Mind…possesses of itself all beauty and poetry, and the power of expressing them. Spirit, God, is heard when the senses are silent.… The influence or action of Soul confers a freedom, which explains the phenomena of improvisation and the fervor of untutored lips" (*Science and Health* 89:20–24). Almost immediately the words of the invocation came to me from phrasings and ideas in the weekly Bible lesson. It came to me to write the invocation the general would want to hear and to discuss the laudable characteristics he expressed with those who worked closest to him.

I was told he insisted that the invocation had to be approved. The prayer I submitted came back quickly with a note, "Great prayer! Approved." Later that day we got another call that instructed us to return the prayer packet because it had been approved by the new chief of staff, and the general wanted the outgoing chief of staff to approve it. Gratefully, it was also approved the second time.

At the rehearsal for the change of command ceremony, the general kept everyone waiting for hours. I finally suggested that the command sergeant major might see if he could get approval for the enlisted soldiers to eat. The officers all stayed in place, and by mid-afternoon the departing general actually appeared.

He walked directly over to me at the first break. He told me he had never seen the prayer himself. He took the prayer from my hands and read it, and I saw him raise his eyebrows toward the end. He mumbled that it was probably longer than his entire change of command speech. He turned to leave, walked a few steps, and then turned back to say, "That's a good prayer. I may have underestimated you." I suspect that was one of the rare times he shared that he had changed his mind about someone. I considered it high praise and a real victory to see this glimmer of humility, and that he'd admit that to me.

On July 31, 1997, we had the change of command ceremony for the V Corps commander. This was the invocation I offered.

Dearest Lord,
Today we would honor a man of common sense and uncommon wisdom, who has remained acutely aware of the common humanity of soldiers, despite our uncommonly demanding profession.

We give You thanks and ask Your blessing on Your servant, [the Lieutenant General and his wife.]

We rejoice that we are equally blessed to receive [a second Lieutenant General and his wife.]

As You impel the progress of these two great soldiers toward rich opportunities, be with them and bless them that all their accomplishments may be to Your glory.

We pray in the name of all that is Holy.   Amen

After paying my respects to the departing general, I proceeded to the Patrick Henry Community Center. I was the very last person to go through the receiving line to greet the new general. When he saw me, he grabbed my hand and shook it. He excitedly exclaimed that my change of command prayer was excellent. As if I wasn't shocked enough, he then began to repeat the opening lines verbatim despite the rather tricky play on the words common and uncommon. That was just the beginning of working for the most affirming leader I ever experienced.

After that my prayers for ceremonies continued to draw heartfelt responses. It became common for people to ask for a copy of the prayer. Families and other colleagues, officers, and friends seemed to be moved by the individual themes and pertinence of the metaphors for the specific persons or groups. Even more telling to me was the number of times a requestor would use the term "uncommonly good," to describe the prayer I'd offer.

I think I was most honored when a young enlisted man approached me after a ceremony and told me he loved the times I did the prayers. He told me he'd never really noted the prayers before because they all seemed pretty much alike. He explained that mine always seemed to be heartfelt and individual. I thank God for His gracious spirit that comes through in prayer when we understand that He is really the true source of the inspiration we need to honor anyone or anything that is part of His creation. We can see them as they are, with great hope in us.

"My prayer, some daily good to do" (a hymn by Mary Baker Eddy, CS Hymnal hymn #253)

While I was the corps chaplain in Heidelberg, Germany, a man from the Pentagon visited my office. He explained that the Women in Military Service for America Memorial would be publicly dedicated at Arlington Cemetery in Washington, DC, in October 1997. The senior women chaplains from each branch of the service were being invited to give invocations at the weeklong activities that preceded the dedication. He asked if I would provide the invocation at the army women's luncheon the day before. I leaped at the opportunity to be a part of that historical week. I distinctly remember the man saying the prayer really needed to be something special.

For over a month I tried to write the invocation. Nothing I wrote seemed good enough. I prayed again about this important duty and finally went to bed the night before thinking I'd try again in the morning. My last prayer of petition was to ask God to help me understand how women had felt about their service.

I woke up at 2:37 AM to find that the words of a poem were coming out of me. Before going to sleep, I had written on every piece of paper in the room at my hotel. I had to take wadded up papers out of the wastebasket and write on the back of the sheets. There wasn't so much as a moment's pause to think of what rhymed with a word or anything. I simply wrote it as a scribe. When I read it afterward, I wept. I knew God, divine Love, had been the source of the wording.

That next morning there was a repeated urging in my thought to leave very early for Andrews Air Force Base. I arrived more than two hours early. When I got to the site, I saw there were tables and chairs filling the entire hanger. I had no idea that that day there would be close to six thousand women who had served in the army. Additional ceremony traffic had become so dense that the chairman of the Joint Chiefs of Staff was going to be late for the ceremony. Once again I expressed my gratitude to God and cataloged another time when obedience to a spiritual intuition had protected me. When you are the first up on the program giving the opening prayer, it isn't acceptable to be late.

I was seated at the head table when General Wilma Vaught came in with General Claudia Kennedy. Their male aides were the only men at the program other than the chairman. A civilian woman sat with us at the head table. Because it had been so loud with six thousand women conversing prior to my invocation, it seemed strikingly quiet as I invited them to pray. This is the invocation that had come to me early that morning.

NOT FOR THE RECOGNITION

Almighty God, in a gentle presence, look on us today,
Help our nation look upon us in a grateful way;
Celebrating "those who served before,"
Leaving only an unsung score.
For before us served a blessed few,

Chaplain (Colonel) Janet Yarlott Horton, US Army (Ret)

Who served without the recognition due;
But did not, nor now do…the duty done for glory…but for You.
For the common Good we serve to heal and renew
The fighting strength for the Red, White and Blue.

We did it because we dare to do, a duty needing done.
Regardless of the sacrifice required—the battle must be won!
We do and did a work inspired, because it was required;
Not in a quest for earthly rewards,
But for the healing support and care
Of fellow soldiers lying there.
Or needing our efforts side by side
To fight for freedom far and wide
That any injustice may not abide.

Knowing only the recognition divine
Was for a selfless unseen goal;
May this celebration make a nation whole,
Who are yet unsure just what's our role.
We simply serve for the task at hand
A quiet sincere and hallowed band;
NOT FOR THE RECOGNITION then nor now.

We seek our enduring obligation
To the Good, the Right, a station
That advances our nation
Toward freedom's goal and a purer vision;
That they might value women there,
A more just record and fair.

What further indication do we need
That women work, fight, and lead
BUT NOT FOR THE RECOGNITION!

Our prayer: For women living and deceased
We ask Your blessings, grace and peace.

Amen

The program proceeded, and it was moving and joyous. When the program was finished, I was moved by the gentle and patient courage of the Chairman of the Joint Chiefs of Staff. He stayed at least two hours, humbly standing for pictures with groups of women. The traffic was still hopelessly snarled, so we all chatted patiently.

One of the male aides came to our table and remarked that this had been a cultural shock for him. He said, "Chaplain, in the last four hours the only time these women were quiet was during your invocation. They even talked non-stop through the chairman's address." I smiled and told him that had shocked me, too. I asked him if you'd have been able to hear a pin drop if this had been a hanger full of men and the chairman had gotten up to speak. He agreed that men would have been stone-cold quiet. The women had talked on. They were only quiet during that invocation.

At that point the civilian woman at the head table said she really loved the invocation and asked if she could have the prayer. I took the wrinkled papers and wrote a copy of it on the back of her bulletin. When I gave the copy to her, she said she wanted the originals. She laughed and explained she was from the Smithsonian Institute. The originals were exactly what she wanted. Then she asked if I would write a letter to her explaining in detail exactly how the prayer had come to me and why it was on the wrinkled papers. I was stunned. I don't think I ever felt more honored in my entire twenty-eight-year career than to think my invocation might have some place in the history of the Women's Memorial. A few days later, General Vaught informed me she posted the invocation on the Women's Memorial web site.

If that wasn't an astounding enough day, the actual ceremony at Arlington Cemetery was a day I will remember forever. Vice President Gore, General Colin Powell, and General Wilma Vaught all spoke about how women were finally going to get at least a token of the recognition due for their service. It wasn't until I was back in Germany that I realized that I was the only speaker whose theme had been that women's contributions weren't motivated by a desire for THE RECOGNITION. Like their fellow soldiers, they were motivated by duty, honor, and love of their country. They were as selfless as all service members who go where they're told and support the missions to stop the killing or make peace. I wanted them to be known as they truly were.

It is only one of three poems I've ever written or maybe I should say transcribed. It still moves me to tears when I read it on anniversary days associated with my military service.

Is it really who you know or to be known "Even as also I am known"

Shortly before I left active duty, I participated in a friend's promotion ceremony. She worked in the secretary of the army's office. There were about fifteen general officers at the ceremony. She was being promoted to full colonel. I was seated in the front row to be able to come forward for the invocation.

As the general conducting the ceremony approached my friend to pin on the eagles, he remarked, "Gwen, this is the last promotion you will receive based on competence." If that wasn't surprising enough, I was completely shocked to hear the two front rows full of general officers laugh exuberantly and applaud. Many other officers attending joined in a shared moment of recognition.

As I thought about what he said, I realized it wasn't merely a comment on the political nature of senior promotions. I also recognized that when an officer being considered for promotion has gone through five previous promotion gates, the pyramid narrows to pretty much the cream of the crop. All the "dead wood" is long gone, and you are competing with highly experienced and bright officers in today's competitive and sophisticated military environment. So to say it comes down to who you know, and who is in and who has fallen out of favor with the highest-ranking officers, is about all that's left. Whether you are in IBM or General Motors or the army, there are only incredibly talented people left, and it depends on who you know.

The only tough part is for those who aren't political and are so involved in their job, quietly doing their work, that they may go unnoticed. I guess only time will tell if we ever come up with the perfectly non-political process of promotions in either the military or larger civilian organizations. The most difficult judgments about promotions have to do with the intangible factors in leadership.

In the army chaplain branch, there are leadership factors that are peculiar to the chaplain corps. Denomination has always been a factor. In its early history, the army chief of chaplains position alternated between Catholic and Protestant chaplains every four years. It wasn't until the constitutionality of the practice was challenged that the denominational alternation was struck down. However, now the pattern has largely changed to a Catholic chief followed by a couple of Protestant chiefs and back to a Catholic chief.

Denomination even among the Protestants is also a big issue. I couldn't count the number of times I was told I had two strikes against me—my gender and my denomination. Many would say the chief is basically a figurehead and see him as the favorite priest or Protestant of the generals in the key positions at the Department of the Army level of leadership. This makes things even more daunting for women who would simply love to be judged on the basis of their systems sense, intelligence, or proven performance.

All the early women chaplains who served pray that as the years advance, our humble beginnings in this regard will make things a little less daunting for those down the road. As I think on this now, my prayer would be that we would be known as Paul refers to it in First Corinthians: to be known as purely as God knows us. That would be perhaps a type of knowing that is kind, just, perfectly accurate, and compassionate. I believe it would be a type of knowing that would be free and unadulterated by prejudice, preconceptions, personal attachment, malice, jealousy, or hatred. If we could get even a step closer to that, there would be a clear measure of progress that included women, and it would benefit all mankind.

CHAPTER 6
ONE GRAND BROTHERHOOD

...my cup runneth over.
"Let brotherly love continue." (Hebrews 13:1)
"It is only with the heart that one can see rightly; what is essential is invisible to the eye....My star will be just one of the stars, for you. And so you will love to watch all the stars in the heavens...They will all be your friends." Antoine De Saint-Exupery in *The Little Prince*
"Alone, we can do so little; together we can do so much."
                                                        Helen Keller

Almost everyone can recall immeasurably sweet moments. Some are childhood memories. Others are situations that didn't start out looking like they would be of the quality they turned out to be. But many of those you'd put in your favorites category. Many times those experiences united people and made us more aware of the fact that we are all children of God. We do have a common humanity, and when that acts to unite us, it blesses everyone involved.

Following will be a few of my favorite times when I felt God's hand powerfully moving people to look beyond themselves to a greater good. It is when we find the love in our hearts to unite that true accomplishments and progress occur.

A Christmas to remember
One bitterly cold Christmas in Michigan, I experienced something that revealed a more profound meaning of the season. Although our family income was quite modest, my mom loved decorating for Christmas. As time passed, she collected enough ornaments to have two trees.

On Christmas Eve my dad came home and immediately began to

pack up one of the trees. He explained that a family whose dad worked for him had just been evicted from their home. They had nothing for Christmas. He had allowed them to move into an abandoned house out at his gravel pit. It had no electricity, and their dad decided they'd make a fire in the fireplace and attempt to sleep there that night. My dad suggested we could all give one of our unopened gifts to the family. We all bundled up and took the whole load out to the family.

In the quiet of the night we knocked on the door. You could initially see the despair in the family's eyes. We said nothing, not wanting to embarrass them in any way. We simply began to set up the tree and place the presents. In the dim light of the small fire, you could see that the children were shyly clinging to their mom. When they realized what we were doing, the mother and children began to weep. We all hugged, and we left.

I always think of that scene when I sing the hymn "O little town of Bethlehem." This line came to me: "How silently, how silently, the wondrous gift is given." Even as a child I realized that the most memorable gifts are given, not received. I believe we lived out the guidance by Mary Baker Eddy, "The rich in spirit help the poor in one grand brotherhood, all having the same Principle, or Father; and blessed is that man who seeth his brother's need and supplieth it, seeking his own in another's good" (*Science and Health* 518:15–19). This experience, this feeling of the brotherhood of man, touched me so deeply I knew I wanted to continue to do whatever I could to comfort God's people when they were in need.

Brothers all

While I was in seminary in the mid-1970s, I worked as an evening security guard in Back Bay Boston in order to pay for food and housing. The first night I worked, after the security foreman had shown me the rounds, it dawned on me I now had to go down dark alleys alone. I had grown up in Iowa, and the idea of doing this in one of the largest cities in the United States seemed daunting to me. I knew I needed to pray and listen for guidance in order to have the courage to do this on a regular basis.

As I walked, I thought about how many psalms lauded the power of God to protect us. A thought came to me with some force: "Would you be afraid if you met Dave or Rick tonight on your rounds?" Dave and

Rick are the names of my two younger brothers, whom I love dearly. I knew I wouldn't be afraid if I saw them. Then it came to me: "Who could you possibly encounter that isn't your brother?" I realized that Paul's letter to the Ephesians helped me understand that there is only "One God and Father of all," as Ephesians 4 says. Then I realized I could do my duty with that sense of protection.

I worked the job for two years and on numerous occasions had to defuse potentially dangerous situations. A man attempted to grab me by the arm and drag me down an alley. He released me when I helped him understand he was a child of God and was pure and kind. When drug dealers with knives chased some children out of the subway, I prayed to know they could feel the power of the Word of God. They froze in their tracks and looked longingly into my eyes, calming instantaneously. They felt God's love and simply retreated back into the MTA. I don't recall feeling afraid because I always felt led and protected by the God I knew was that great!

A new look at the 10 Commandments

In 1977 the military was attempting to be more responsive to families. They hadn't been before; for many years sergeants would joke that if the army wanted you to have a family, they would have issued you one. The chaplains at Fort Sill, Oklahoma, offered workshops on family support for the basic trainees' wives. It was there I decided a truly exceptional case would be that rare time I'd lend someone money.

Officers in the very public battalion parking lot laughed at me when they saw a woman family member asking me for $20. She approached me explaining that she had put water in her gas tank, thinking that would make the gas go farther. I explained how bad that was for the car and not to do it again. She told me she had no money for the baby's formula or food for the children until her husband would get his first paycheck in a week or so. I took her to get diapers and formula from a military food closet and told her I would lend her the twenty. I suggested she might return it only if they could. If not, I would consider it a gift.

When I reentered the battalion headquarters, the officers and NCOs who saw me give her the money laughed at me and told me to kiss the money good-bye. I countered with authority that I didn't wish to be any part of stealing anyone's God-given dignity, nor did I wish to bear false witness against my neighbor. I mentioned that I only knew of one Creator, so this family must really be God's children. I continued that I was trusting that God was helping the family, who were simply new to the army. What they needed was an opportunity to get on their feet financially. I had been struck by the sincerity of this woman, who insisted so vehemently that she and her husband always paid their debts.

It was a number of weeks before the young private graduated from basic training and had finally gotten his first couple of paychecks. He came to the battalion headquarters walking hand in hand with his daughter and son, while his wife held their baby. Because he was so new to the army, he didn't realize he could've talked to me in the privacy of my office. So he simply sat down in the crowded battalion clerk's office in full view of many officers and NCOs and took out a baby's sock. It was the kind you see with the little lace edging on it. This caught everyone's attention. He began to take coins out of the sock and dutifully count out his first installment of $5 towards paying their debt. He carefully stacked the coins in piles. They were mostly dimes, nickels, and pennies. He kept insistently proclaiming, "I always pay my debts!" There was not a single dry eye in the hallway or surrounding office areas.

I choked back my tears and told him I understood he and his family were only starting out. Because he was very insistent, I agreed I would accept this first payment. Then I made a suggestion on how to pay the other payments. I told him he could save the five dollars in the sock three more times. The first time he could buy something the baby needed. The second time he could buy something his daughter needed, and then something his son needed the final time. If he would consider each one a gift from me, then I would consider the debt paid. Only after I was very insistent did he agree that he could accept those terms. I hugged his wife and the kids and they left.

There was a gentle atmosphere in the headquarters that day. It seemed the NCOs became very special allies for me after that. I think they appreciated an officer standing up for an enlisted man's integrity so boldly.

The Army salutes the Navy

In 1978 when I was at Fort Sill, I participated in a retreat in Maine. A rather senior navy officer openly expressed that he was radically against women being in the military. Surprisingly, he asked me to discuss his concerns over lunch. We had a kind and sincere exchange. He even seemed moved by some experiences I shared with him.

That afternoon, one of the instructors wanted to illustrate the power of non-verbal communication. He asked if anyone wanted to volunteer to give an example. I jumped at the opportunity and walked across the room. Very respectfully, I came to a position of attention in front of the navy officer. He rose to his feet. Then I ceremoniously saluted him. The room became very hushed, and you could see the impact on him and others in the training. He was so moved he had tears in his eyes. He slowly and respectfully returned the salute. Quietly, he reached out to me and gave me a heartfelt hug.

It may not be words that are the most persuasive when emotions run high. However, when respect and sincerity touch a person's heart, there can be a more pronounced movement in thought and a feeling of camaraderie.

A silent call for help

After a long day at the Pentagon in 1992, I was not thrilled to see that the subway had been stopped. Police were clearing a suicide scene. Things finally seemed to be wrapping up when the public address system informed us the first car would arrive in just a few minutes. People began to crush even closer to the edge of the platform, hoping to be first to capitalize on the restored train service. I prayed that God would give everyone the ideas they needed to get things back on track (pardon the pun!). I knew the Bible assured us, "God shall supply all your need according to his riches" (Philippians 4:19).

About that time, my thought was drawn to a woman who had a baby in a backpack. I noticed she seemed very distressed and that she had a red and white cane in her hand. I worked my way over to her and asked if she needed help. She choked out that she had not been able to use a toilet for hours and she also really needed to get the baby home. I offered to take her up through the mob of people and find a nearby restaurant with a restroom. She blinked back tears and said she just wanted to get on the train she could hear slowly making its way into the station.

I took her arm and began asking people to let her come to the front of the track. I was in my "speak with authority" mode. Once they realized she was not sighted, they made way for her and the baby. I escorted her onto the first train through a crush of people inside. I ordered two people sitting in the seats reserved for the handicapped to help her get the baby out of her baby carrier and give her one of the seats. Two people alertly jumped to her assistance, and she was in a seat with the baby on her lap in just moments.

I stepped off the train, and several people thanked me for being aware and assisting her. Two marines in uniform approached me. One said to me, "You're a real take-charge kind of person. You should be in the military!" I told them proudly, "I am!" They came to a position of attention and saluted me. It was so heartwarming to see that these marines realized a woman should be in the military and also what a good thing an act of kindness is.

One grand brotherhood

One of the secretaries at the Pentagon forwarded all our phones to my boss's office in the outer "E" ring in 1992. Unaware she had done so, I missed the call from the man I rehearsed Sunday service with on Thursday evenings at our church. He also worked in the District, and rehearsing after work saved me driving a hundred extra miles back and forth to our church in Virginia from Annapolis. He assumed I'd forgotten or got called away. He had no escort, so he had to leave.

After waiting a considerable time, I discovered the phone problem. I was tempted initially to be frustrated about the mistake. I caught myself and recalled what I told a chaplain earlier that month. I proclaimed my sincere faith that God doesn't make a mistake. I knew that as Readers we had desired to be obedient to the requirement to practice each service. I declared that the Bible assured us God blesses the obedient. I concluded that what seemed to be a mistake on the surface must actually have a purpose. I started driving home, and a passage from that week's Bible lesson included the gospel recognition that God's eye is on the sparrow. A related study passage from our textbook also assured me, "The rich in spirit help the poor in one grand brotherhood, all having the same Principle, or Father; and blessed is that man who seeth his brother's need and supplieth it, seeking his own in another's good" (*Science and Health* 518:15–19).

As I got into Annapolis, I drove by a gas station close to my home. I felt an overwhelming urge to turn into the station. Initially, I kept arguing myself out of it. I had just filled the tank that morning and had only driven to the Pentagon and back. However, that inner voice of Love was insistent that I should get gas again.

I wasn't going to fail to be obedient to such a persistent intuition. I gave the cashier a pre-payment of a twenty-dollar bill. The tank was so full I was only able to pump a couple gallons of gas. (In 1993 that was less than three dollars.) Standing in line to pay, I noticed a young girl and her mother were talking with the attendant. The woman's young daughter had not cleared the pump and had been unable to get the gas to dispense. The cashier was insistent on charging them for gas they never received. He stubbornly stated he was keeping the woman's only five-dollar bill.

She was weeping, attempting to explain that was all the money she had. She had only wanted two dollars of gas because she needed food for dinner. The cashier was unrelenting and condescending.

I asked the man in the booth if there was any reason he couldn't give her my change. He retorted I could do anything I wanted to with my change. He shoved my seventeen dollars and change at her. She was genuinely overcome. Both she and her daughter wept. She insisted it was too much. I assured her it was a gift from God. She said she had church that night and would thank God for providing the manna. Her little daughter threw her arms around my waist and asked if I was an angel. She exclaimed with joy that they would be able to eat that night.

I drove home expressing gratitude for the grander sense of brotherhood we had felt. I was on my knees mentally. God understood there was a way to meet His little one's needs.

Some communications are divine

I was involved about 1998 in a very important Warfighter exercise in Grafenwoehr, Germany. These exercises prepared us for yet another Balkan deployment. Things started badly, and people were delayed by bad weather. There had been a suicide in one of our units just prior to our departure. The complex pieces of communications technology weren't working. The soldiers running them were in the unit where the suicide had occurred. They knew me because I had been with them for the memorial service.

One young private sought me out on the command ramp. That's an area where the generals and senior officers normally have their work sections. It took a lot of courage for him to come there. I could tell he was nervous but also upset as he approached me. On that dark rainy evening he implored me, "Ma'am, would you think it sacrilegious if I asked you to pray over the Single Channel Tactical Satellite?" I said I'd be happy to pray with him and his section, although I knew nothing about the communications equipment. However, what I did know was that God loved the humble and sincere seekers for Truth. And we had every right to ask God's guidance to bless everyone involved.

We hustled through the pouring rain to the site where his team was feverishly attending to the equipment. When his lieutenant saw I was a colonel, he began to apologize to me for the private bothering me. I gently told him I couldn't think of anything more important than what they were doing for our exercise. I assured him they could never be wrong in asking for prayer.

They all seemed very frustrated and said nothing they tried would bring the communications on line. They were diligently examining each piece and gauge. I told the soldiers we needed a new spiritual perspective on the situation. I began by affirming there could be no penalty for doing their duty.

At that point we bowed our heads in prayer. It felt so genuine that I knew God was letting us know he was with us. We prayed to understand what makes the fear and frustration go away. We talked about the fact that we weren't praying for a machine so much as praying about our need to have a sense of harmony. We affirmed that a machine couldn't rob us of our peace. We agreed we'd simply asked God for a right idea for operating the machine. Immediately, I thought of a Bible verse from Proverbs 3: "Trust in the Lord with all thine heart; and lean not unto thine own understanding. In all thy ways acknowledge him, and he shall direct thy paths." That passage spoke to the moment perfectly. The soldiers' fear and frustration visibly melted away. They thanked me profusely, and I returned to the command briefing van.

The prayer calmed a sea of unneeded frustration. The peace that replaced the anxiety and fear must have helped them to see things that may have been right in front of them all along. In prayer we seek that deep and holy meaning of our favorite scriptures, with all our heart and with all our soul. It was the love the soldiers felt for all the people they were seeking to bless that had an extraordinarily calming effect.

In just a few minutes the V Corps signal officer came into the van for the commander's briefing. For the first few days, the signal officer would put up a slide full of bubbles that represented each key signal asset. They had all previously been red to denote none were functioning. He pulled up his slide and triumphantly announced that all the communications gear was working. The entire slide was green bubbles.

The chief of staff was so impressed with the complete reversal of the impasse that he asked what happened. With great gusto the signal officer announced to the entire video teleconference that the chaplain had prayed for the communications team, and all the communications equipment had started working. I added that the signal crews had faithfully worked to find all the right fixes. The chief chimed in and said if anyone else was having problems in their areas they should call the corps chaplain.

That experience set the tone for the rest of the exercise. The chief had us start with a chaplain slide each day, called the Thought of the Day. It had a famous quote that spoke to a leadership concept and set the tone for the day. People expressed their gratitude for the productive atmosphere it had established first thing in the morning. It's always a blessing when we see God's purpose in our day.

A little levity leavens the whole lump

On a field exercise at Grafenwoehr, Germany, in that time around 1998, there was a shortage of billeting. I was given a bunk with the male officers in one large open bay. That wasn't a big deal because we all dressed and did our morning preparation in the male and female bathrooms across the road.

The first morning, as our signal battalion commander was waking up, he sat up at the opposite end of the barracks in a top bunk. He playfully hurled an insult my way, knowing everyone would hear it. I saw this as a good sign because they all playfully insulted each other. It was a sign that you were "one of the guys." He challenged me, "Chaplain Horton, you look terrible in the morning!" I knew this was not a moment to show any shred of weakness. So, not to be outdone, I volleyed back, "So what's your excuse for the rest of the day?" The guys were in my court as they laughed and hurled their own insults at him about his ugly mug. It was one of those dear moments you get kidded about because you're the little sister and they're your brothers in arms. It was just one of life's moments that sweetens the cup you drink.

The Fort Leavenworth Buffalo Soldier statue

When we were on that same exercise, a young major I worked with told me about a poignant experience he had at Fort Leavenworth, Kansas. He asked me if I could help him understand what it really meant. Before arriving, he'd heard about a statue dedicated to celebrate the contributions of the Buffalo Soldiers. He explained that the U.S. Congress authorized the formation of several black regiments in 1866, mostly to go west. Black soldiers had first served, honorably and in several units, during the Civil War, and the army confidently recruited and organized its "Negro troops" to tame the west. White officers commanded. The term Buffalo Soldier was coined by Native Americans when they first saw the all-black Tenth Cavalry Regiment out of Fort Leavenworth.

My young friend had never seen even a picture of the statue of the Buffalo Soldier, but it's an amazing work of art depicting a proud soldier on a spirited horse rearing up on its hind legs. The grace and beauty of this work of art had astounded him. As a black officer, this sight struck a deep chord in his heart as he crested a hill and it came into view across a pond. Before he realized what he'd done, he found he had gotten out of his car.

This statue is on the major thoroughfare through Fort Leavenworth. It was peak morning traffic. The Post Exchange, the grocery commissary, and the childcare center are on that road. Command and General Staff College students, faculty, and family members all arrive each morning on this one road.

He found himself transfixed for several moments, taking in its impact on him and the moments of history it represented. All at once he realized what he'd done. There was a tear running down his cheek. He turned around to see that traffic in both directions had stopped. Now, he had not impeded traffic in the other direction whatsoever, but traffic in all lanes had stopped, perfectly silent. Not one person honked a horn. Not one person yelled at him. They just soaked in what he was experiencing, allowing him to turn around and very quietly get in his car and drive off.

More than a year later, he was still wondering what had happened there. I listened a moment and asked him if he thought something universal had united those people on the road that day. I proposed that it was a shared moment of recognition and gratitude, not just for the striking beauty of the statue, but also for what it means to minority officers who served today. This shared recognition had united many different people that day. He agreed heartily, and he seemed deeply moved once again.

I shared a passage from our textbook with him: "One infinite God, good, unifies men and nations; constitutes the brotherhood of man; ends wars; [and] fulfils the Scripture, 'Love thy neighbor as thyself.'" (*Science and Health* 340:23–25).

This type of unity and sense of brother or sisterhood with all beings comes to bless us whenever it comes into our thought. At times like that, it is often felt by others as we experience it here and now in our lives. It is truly humbling to be any part of bringing it to bear in our world. I always asked God to let my work as a chaplain reflect even the most modest crumbs of that heavenly manna he gives to mankind, when they "hunger and thirst after righteousness." It is this principle of love which constitutes one grand brotherhood that unifies all mankind.

CHAPTER 7
WHEN THE HOLY SPIRIT SPEAKS
THERE IS HEALING

The Lord is my shepherd, I shall not want...Surely goodness and mercy shall follow me all the days of my life:
"And these signs shall follow them that believe…they shall lay hands on the sick, and they shall recover." (Mark 16:17, 18)
"Spirit, God, is heard when the senses are silent." (*Science and Health* 89:20–21)

When the Holy Spirit speaks, it is often a gentle, still small voice that speaks to the heart. It embraces all those who are hungering and thirsting to understand what it means to love God and love your neighbor. It goes where most fear to tread. God's presence acknowledged, felt, and praised is one of the most powerful experiences a person can have. It heals because of its genuine nature and its all-inclusiveness.

In your life and your career there are always high points. You cherish the fact that the road included moments of holy, uplifting inspiration. These experiences are varied and often include people of many differing traditions, family members, and friends. The purity of the love they expressed in their neighbors' time of need or when the need was great yielded healing. It was a love that united, blessed, and healed all involved in these many instances. Love knows no bounds. The one thing that is common is that genuine, compassionate love convinces like nothing else. Yet, there are times that it's met with doubt or even fear. However, that doesn't make it any less true or current or powerful. For me these experiences were instructive. I hope these demonstrations of the presence of the Holy Spirit will awaken recognition in others who have felt such love.

No foul, no harm

In 1971 when I was a young woman working as a summer recreation counselor, I had a most inspiring healing. My co-counselor and I were scheduled to show a movie to all the city parks program participants at an alternate location, away from our normal site. One of the mothers dropped her two small children at our customary school location. As we drove by, we saw the girls standing at the school alone.

I immediately turned in and told them we'd drive them to the correct location. I put them in my back seat and reached back from the driver's seat and slammed the door firmly. I remember thinking with two little ones in the back I should be sure the door closed securely. As it closed I realized my hand was in the door.

I knew instantly I needed to turn to God for a more harmonious sense of what was happening. I did this so quickly that I declared a vigorous "NO!" In the quiet of my thought, I firmly denied any suggestion that there could be an accident in God's kingdom or any infringement on God's law of harmony. I remember affirming that it was out of love for the children and concern for their safety that I had gone to their aid. I couldn't think there could have possibly been any sin in that motive or the corresponding actions. I couldn't imagine that if God is Love, as the Epistle of I John affirms, that there should be any punishment for kind consideration. I intentionally didn't look at or attempt to closely examine the wound. There was a cloth on the floor, so I quickly wrapped it around my hand to contain the bleeding.

My co-counselor was very upset because of the blood and the severity of what seemed to have happened. However, I immediately asked her not to speak, explaining with great authority that I needed to pray. I affirmed the scriptural command in the first chapter of Genesis that man was made in the image and likeness of God, Spirit. I reasoned that matter was not that likeness. I absolutely immersed myself in the sense of God's omnipotence and omnipresence.

Suddenly, it came to me we had a room full of kids waiting for a movie. I quickly drove to the main city park. It wasn't until we stopped to change the second reel of the movie that my co-counselor said, "I'm sorry. I can't shut up any longer. I want to see what's happened to your hand." That was the first time I had thought of it again for over an hour. Shocked, I looked at one hand and then the other. Neither of us could identify even a single mark on either hand.

My co-counselor was confused because she wasn't seeing any wound, and that she had also seen the blood on my hand, the cloth, and door. The healing was particularly comprehensive because I had no memory of even a moment of pain. It helped me understand God's law of harmony was a very present possibility right here, right now! I can say with the deepest gratitude that I have seen God's greatness and His love for His children.

The wonder of the Amana colonies

In 1972 in central Iowa, as a religious studies student, I studied the religion of the Amana Colonies, the Communities of True Inspiration. Oddly, I found my being a Christian Scientist was equally interesting to my fellow students and members of the colonies. In fact, I found I was answering questions late into the night for most of the first week. By the weekend, I could barely speak.

While I was shopping on Saturday, a woman in a fabric store remarked that I had better get to a doctor because of my voice. I kindly informed her I relied on prayer for healing. This seemed to incense her, and she came back at me with great force. She insisted that God had made doctors. I thanked her for her concern, but she kept at me and began to try to force her opinion on me. I stopped her and told her that her logic was faulty. I told her that some humans make the choice to sell cars, while others make the choice to sell guns. I added that by her logic one would have to infer that God made thieves or gamblers or "bookies," also. Where I would agree that God made all of mankind, I didn't believe I could infer that he had made their humanly designed and chosen professions or job categories. She walked away brusquely, and we left the store.

A fellow student who was with me heard the intense discussion and asked me to get a soda with her in the nearby snack bar. The woman's remark had sparked yet more questions in her thought. I was so concerned about wanting to answer her many continuing questions about healing that I turned to God with my whole heart to find the strength to respond to her request. It came to me in a compelling wave of gratitude: "There is nothing that I love more than sharing God's Word with seekers for Truth." I was simply being a transparency for this dear one who wanted to know about God's greatness and love. That wasn't anything that required effort on my part. I was simply the vehicle. That couldn't possibly result in any strain on my part.

By the time we sat down with sodas, my friend had yet another question. As I answered it, I felt a great sense of gratitude for all I had learned from the Bible. Suddenly, she realized my voice was strong and clear, when it had been barely audible for the whole day. She nearly jumped across the table, embracing me with both arms. She exclaimed in a very exuberant and joyous squeal, "You're healed! You're healed! I've seen it with my own eyes! Now I understand what you've been explaining to us." Gratitude is a very important part of many healings. We had a tremendously productive time in our studies there, and the sense of harmony and friendship with the Amana families was deeply rewarding. The presence of the Holy Spirit in everyday life is tangible in human experience.

Mutual appreciation replaces condemnation

In my last year of seminary in Boston, 1976, I was warned that a required senior seminar instructor didn't understand our religion and would often confront our church's students during the class sessions. I found his attacks were pointed and frequent. Other students began to comment on the viciousness of the attacks. Because this often resulted in sincere discussions with students after class about Christian healing, I believe I was unaware that it was still sparking some resentment in my own thought.

The next weekend I was invited to chaperone a youth skiing trip in New Hampshire. Having grown up in Iowa, I'd never skied before. The conditions were quite icy and not ideal for new skiers. I found myself cartwheeling down a slope. I realized after I picked myself up that I was unable to move one of my arms. I was grateful that my immediate thoughts of God's omnipotence had completely healed any sense of pain.

On Monday the weekly Bible lesson contained a wonderful passage from Paul's letter to the Romans: "There is therefore now no condemnation to them which are in Christ Jesus, who walk not after the flesh, but after the Spirit" (Romans 8:1). I felt this biblical promise meant that there was no cause for the instructor's condemnation of me—nor was it right for me to feel any sense of condemnation for him. I had to stand on the fact we were both children of God.

Just before the seminar, another student noticed I couldn't move my arm. She predicted his attacks might be even worse. I shared with her what the scripture had meant to me that morning and that I was expecting a healing. She originally thought I meant a physical healing of the arm. I explained to her that that would be wonderful, but the essential part of the healing would be so much more. The healing of the suggestion of condemnation was far more important. The issues of the heart held more magnitude for me. I insisted that the love I had felt was a healing of the heart. I explained that a physical healing is more like a by-product of the more essential moral and spiritual progress. She delighted in that comment and remarked with great joy, "Oh, now I get it. You can't heal someone you don't love."

We entered the classroom a few moments later. She was helping me take off my coat when the instructor became aware that I wasn't able to move my arm. This seemed to outrage him instantly. He crossed the room and got up in my face. He began by loudly and severely condemning me for my beliefs. He accused me of pretending evil was nothing and then doing nothing when I was hurting. Because my heart was ready, I became very aware for the first time that he wouldn't be so upset if he didn't care. I felt a deep sense of love for him and an abiding recognition of God's presence right there. As these truths flooded my thought, I found myself reaching out and putting my hands on his shoulders. With conviction and authority I lovingly assured him, "I'm not doing nothing. I'm doing the most powerful thing you can possibly do—I'm praying!" At that moment we all heard a crunching sound. With delight I began to move my arm and noticed even the discoloration had disappeared instantly. He rejoiced, "I've seen it with my own eyes. Now I know why it is essential to see evil as nothing."

Where he had previously fought the idea of me writing my final thesis paper on the concept of evil as nothing, he then insisted that I must write the paper on that exact idea. He awarded me an A on the paper and wrote a comment explaining that it had caused him to rethink his entire theology. The experience had enabled me to let go of my condemnation and see it for its worthlessness.

The gas chamber: Our fiery furnace in chaplain basic training

Early in 1976, while I was still in seminary in Boston, I found I was absolutely terrified by the thought of going into the tear gas chamber in my summer Army Chaplain Officer Basic Course. I had heard the "war stories" of those who had experienced the gas chamber and its toxic effect on your eyes and breathing. I knew I needed to pray diligently to meet these aggressive suggestions of fear immediately.

I spent some time praying about what to pray about. I quietly listened, and the direction was very clear. I felt led to study the Bible story of Shadrach, Meshach, and Abednego being thrown into the fiery furnace and Moses experiencing a bush that burned but wasn't consumed. I also studied a chapter on how to pray to stop animal magnetism (an old world name for hypnotism) in our denominational textbook. I made a commitment to study these passages once a day for two months. They were so inspiring that I found I would sometimes look at them as frequently as three times a day.

It was one of the most amazing periods in my life. From the Bible I was learning about how lovingly the Hebrew slaves faced the fire and how Moses was obedient to do what God told him to do. I learned how tempting it was to accept that the repeated stories meant a challenging thing had to be dreaded. I saw how these holy people had seen these threats as a joyous opportunity to experience God's presence with them in times of need.

I must have been so filled with the joy of the Holy Spirit that people would come up to me and say, "I don't know why I'm saying this to you, but could you tell me about Christian Science?" At other times someone would ask if I could help him or her understand something in the Bible. By that summer I had forgotten why I had started the study, and I continued to pray this way for about six months. It wasn't until I was walking into the gas chamber that I remembered why I had begun the study.

Officers with combat specialties conducted the tear gas mask confidence exercise. Our class was a very large class. Since my maiden name was Yarlott, I was in the last group to go into the chamber. The whole idea of the exercise is to learn confidence that the mask will protect you, if you keep it on—therefore, they make you take it off in the tear gas chamber! You're required to say your name, rank, social security number, and the state you grew up in, to force you to inhale the gas.

All the prior service men that helped the cadre were in my group. The officer conducting the drill threw a lot more gas crystals on the fire, and the gas cloud became very thick in the chamber. They warned our group, "You thought you were going to get off easy because you helped us, but we're really going to get you."

I was immersed in the joyous thought I'd done my prayer and I'd get to do this now! I had no sense of fear. I was ready to apply what I had been studying in the Christian Science textbook. A phrase from *Science and Health* that encourages you not to be hypnotized by the repetition of bad things held in front of you came to my thought: "Mind-science is wholly separate from any half-way impertinent knowledge, because Mind-science is of God and demonstrates the divine Principle, working out the purposes of good only" (*Science and Health* 103:12-15). That was precisely what I needed to understand for that moment. I knew God governed the universe as divine Love, and He never had ordained a law to harm or inflict His children. I felt God's presence with me. I knew I couldn't be separated from Him. It was as if He were my armor and protective shield from any harm. I felt like I was looking down on the experience, wholly separate from any human sense of being in the chamber. I felt a clarity of thought as I heard a Bible precept—that my life was "hid with Christ in God" (Colossians 3:3).

We were told to remove our gas masks. Because the gas was so thick, even the prior service guys were choking and blinded by the density of the gas. They were literally in a pile attempting to get out the door. I stood still and calmly said all my information. Once the instructors had pulled the men apart, they were able to get the door open. I hadn't left the chamber because the cadre hadn't given us the order that we could leave the chamber.

One of the majors walked back into the chamber. He had his mask on and stared at me just standing quietly—unmasked. I was reveling in gratitude that I had no reaction to the tear gas. Finally, the instructor said through his mask, "Humor me and go outside?" Once we were out the door, he took off his mask and said, "I have to ask you a question. What were you doing in there?" In complete joy I replied, "I was praying." Then, he said, "Are you a Christian Scientist?" I nodded my head. After a silence he said, "That's really something. You know, I've been here four years, and I have never had a single class when not one person got ill until now." I was even more grateful for that. Your prayer is rarely ever limited to only your needs. It often blesses the people around you.

Chaplain (Colonel) Janet Yarlott Horton, US Army (Ret)

The Holy Spirit saves the day at our team spirit training exercise in Korea

In Korea in 1980, I found a young soldier in the Second Infantry Division who was also a Christian Scientist. Our Air Force chaplain had identified two Christian Scientist airmen in his area south of Seoul. With great joy, two of us were planning to attend the only Christian Science lecture that would be given during our year in Korea. Miss Jane Robbins would be speaking at the Christian Science Society in Seoul.

The infantry private and I were tempted to be disappointed when we found that our division's major field exercise would be that same week. We knew that meant we would be in a remote field site about three hours south of Seoul with no transportation.

I talked with the young soldier and told him we wouldn't yield to discouragement. We agreed that we would pray in support of the lecture. I told him that wherever he was on the exercise that day, I would find him, and I suggested that we could read our weekly Bible lesson together. We knew there had to be a right idea for this day and that we would be led to find our part in valuing the Christian message being offered to that country that had so lovingly embraced us.

When that day arrived, I tracked him down. We had just sat down on some rocks and opened the Bible when our assistant division commander, a brigadier general, came through the area to view the exercise. He knew me by my first name because I had helped him work a couple of very sensitive issues shortly after arriving in Korea. He asked what we were doing. I explained that today the only Christian Science lecture of the year was being held in Seoul. I added we were praying and reading in support of the lecture.

He asked when it would start. I told him in about an hour. He got the biggest smile on his face and said he was just leaving for a quick meeting in Seoul. He invited us to fly there in his helicopter, as he had unfilled seats. The private was nervous and told the general he didn't think his sergeant would approve his leaving the exercise. The general smiled kindly and tapped the star he wore on his uniform. He assured the young man that he would inform our commanders he was taking us. He felt it was important for us to attend this singular religious opportunity. He also assured our commanders he would have us back in about three to four hours.

As we landed in Seoul, we saw the air force chaplain and his enlisted men getting into his car. He was in the perfect place to give us a ride directly to the lecture. I suspect this was one of the few times Miss Robbins had a young soldier with an M-16 rifle in the front row of her talk. Our field gear and camouflaged faces seemed perfectly appropriate when she illustrated one point about healing with a story about being a bush pilot in Alaska. We loved the lecture, thanked the speaker, and drove back just in time to connect with the general as he came out of his meeting. We were back at our field site in about four hours.

The presence of the Holy Spirit was evident in each event that day. Each step was perfectly timed by our heavenly Father. God had put in place everything we needed and surrounded us with expressions of love and perfect logistical support the entire day. Healing can be the recognition of harmony when everything else might say it's impossible.

"We have…an house not made with hands, eternal in the heavens." (II Corinthians 5:1)

Everyone in the military is required to submit to physical examinations about every five years. Because my practice was to rely on prayer for healing, I didn't have any other documents in my military medical record. In order to be cleared to continue to participate in daily physical fitness training, I reported for a special over-forty medical screening. These medical experiences were always a bit embarrassing to me, and I always prayed specifically before reporting. I prayed to counter my discomfort with the idea that it could be just the reverse. I could express joy and even look forward to the day's activities. I began to see there was no reason it couldn't be an opportunity to share my faith in God's constant care for me.

At each office in the Pentagon medical clinic, it seemed something interesting happened. When I reported to the designated start point, the receptionist told me I should tell my boss it was the correct reporting area. I told the woman I wasn't doing recon for my boss; I was there to take the required over-forty physical. She told me I looked way too young and asked me to verify my birth year. That didn't hurt my feelings in the least and got things started off on a great note.

At every station I reported to, I expressed gratitude that the people were remarkably kind and quick. I kept focused on the spiritual idea that there really had only been one examination, and that was in the first chapter of Genesis: "And God saw everything that he had made, and, behold, it was very good." I held in my thought the highest standard. God's children were made in [His] image and likeness, as it establishes at the beginning of Genesis. I prayed to see myself the way St. Paul spoke of our existence. I figured if someone had to see me unclothed, then it would be in the sense spoken of in II Corinthians. I took the epistle at its word—"We have a building of God, an house not made with hands, eternal in the heavens"—and it assured me I could "be absent from the body, and…be present with the Lord" (II Corinthians 5:1, 8). I affirmed that this spiritual identity spoken of in the Bible was all that could be seen.

A few weeks later I was asked to return for a complex readout of the "risk assessment." I was surprised to see an entire panel of doctors. The woman doctor who was the head of the Pentagon clinic explained they had never had an officer receive a nearly perfect score on the assessment. The lead doctor started by saying, "You're in amazing shape. You must exercise all the time and eat right." The doctor said they'd never seen someone with a perfect EKG, a 131 cholesterol reading, a perfect chest X-ray, etc. The nutritionist began by asking me what I ate for breakfast. I told her I didn't really eat breakfast or lunch. I explained I ate M&Ms, potato chips, and a soda at about 10:30 in the morning. She laughed and said, "No, really, what do you eat?" I reiterated that I really did eat that same snack each day. I told them they could ask anyone who had served with me. She continued to press me and asked what I ate for dinner. I told her I ate whatever I wanted to. She asked about red meat. I told her I loved it and especially liked the fat on the Iowa beef I'd grown up eating. She pressed me again and again until she closed her notebook and stated, "You defy every nutritional law." She asked how I'd explain my unorthodox eating habits in such striking distinction to my healthy scores on all the tests. I said, "I neither fear nor worship my food." I explained that I trusted that the Bible assured us that it isn't what goes into a man's mouth that defiles him, but it is what comes out of it that we needed to be most attentive to (Matthew 15:11). The panel seemed baffled but thought about the idea.

They asked me about my workout regime. I told them I only did the three exercises required on the army physical fitness test and that was because that was the army's expectation. I told them I had always been able to do any distance running my units required. They asked how far I had run. I told them I ran two miles in basic training and had no problem immediately running six and a half miles with my first unit. It seemed incredible to them that I did that with no soreness or negative physical repercussions. At that point they asked me why I thought I defied all of the normal physical rules. I told them for me it was a matter of daily specific prayer. They stopped the interview and stated there was nothing they could learn from me.

The doctor in charge of the Pentagon medical clinic was the only one who didn't leave. She asked how she might study this manner of prayer. I told her I would bring her a Bible and a copy of our denominational textbook, *Science and Health with Key to the Scriptures*. She asked if I could get them to her by 7:30 the next morning, which I gladly did. I never saw her again, but this wouldn't be the last time I was grilled by the doctor performing an army physical.

A Methodist minister, a Mormon chaplain, and a Christian Scientist walked into a healing!

While serving in Heidelberg, Germany, I made many a drive to and from the army training center at Grafenwoehr. My planner chaplain or my deputy corps chaplain would often ride with me. The four-hour drives seemed to go very quickly when we'd get involved in some deeper discussions of our religious beliefs. In 1997 a young Mormon chaplain and I talked extensively about our understanding of God and in great detail about healing prayer. I had many opportunities to share the detail of various experiences of healing. The young man's questions were sincere and showed a genuine desire to understand more about Christian healing. I had studied the Book of Mormon, and he often helped me understand his tradition better.

The next year I had a new planner who was a Methodist minister. He also asked questions at great lengths, showing he too was yearning to understand more about healing prayer. We also had numerous opportunities to share while driving to duty stations.

The year after I left Europe, the Methodist chaplain returned to a chaplain training conference limping badly on one foot. He remarked to his friend, the Mormon chaplain who had also been my planner, that this sprain was worse than a previous sprain. He lamented that he wasn't able to run for several weeks with the lesser sprain. The Mormon remarked that it was too bad Chaplain Horton wasn't there, or he could've asked for a prayer treatment that would heal the foot. Then the two began to discuss that perhaps they could remember from their talks with me how to apply the healing prayer concepts themselves.

One of them remembered that I always prayed while I was running. They both agreed it was not so much about the foot or ankle as it was about what had been on the young chaplain's heart as he ran. They recalled Bible passages that supported the need to search your heart and your mind. They agreed he must identify if there had been anything unholy he was entertaining in his thought when running. The chaplain had to admit he'd been a bit prideful and had been congratulating himself that he was a better runner than some of the combat arms planners. They also agreed they needed to affirm that they could trust God to be able and willing to heal those who love Him and sought His guidance on such occasions. They agreed to love their neighbor as themselves and keep clearly in thought a purer motive for this activity and determined in the future they would also be praying and praising God while running. They also agreed they felt very humbled. By the next day, the chaplain was elated he could walk more freely. He was back running within a very short period of time, rather than the number of weeks he originally feared would be the case because of the severity of the injury.

These are the times we understand what it means to be brothers and sisters in Christ. It is not at all surprising that such incredible humility, loving kindness, and a sense of unity would produce healing results.

A house and a prayer: "…I will dwell in the house of the Lord for ever"
When I was due to leave Germany in 2000, I couldn't get orders for a new assignment in the Department of Defense. It was tempting to be overwhelmed, resentful, or anxious when thirteen other officers on the corps staff had their orders early. They all had time to take administrative leave granted for house hunting. Horror stories from each one told of similar difficulties and seemed to confirm the Washington, DC, area market was out of control. Many told of bidding wars against ten to fifteen other buyers.

My orders didn't arrive until the third week of April for a June 7 rotation. The week we flew, I was encouraged by the sixth verse of the Twenty-Third Psalm, "I will dwell in the house of the Lord for ever." I told my husband not to worry. We would find "the house of the Lord," the house that would bless us. I knew God would indeed prepare the way for us.

The first day back we investigated rentals. The few that were left were properties that had not been maintained or were not located in areas considered to be safe. In mid-afternoon on Friday it was as if I could see in my mind where we should look. I told my husband where to drive and to turn into an area directly across the street from the Vienna, Virginia, Metro stop. We were copying down a number on a For Sale sign when a realtor stopped and asked if we'd like to see the townhouse across the street. She remarked that she would have missed us if we had been even one or two minutes later. She had just picked up an adjacent property and hadn't even had time to list it. It was a well-maintained property, and we immediately put in a bid. She cautioned us to keep looking over the weekend and predicted there would be a bidding war.

That weekend, as we waded through the other people also looking at the few homes still on the market, the realtor called us. She told my husband she had gotten busy with an open house and had not put in our bid. She asked us to meet her at her office on Monday. The realtor in the house we were looking at overheard the discussion and noted my husband's shock. He told Jeff that if she hadn't submitted our bid, it was illegal, and she could lose her license. I resisted the fear or annoyance that might have caused us to conclude this was wrong. I kept getting a sense of assurance that it was part of God's plan and was a necessary event, and He would bless everyone involved.

On Monday, although the owner had a number of other offers, the realtor told us she wanted the lady chaplain to have the property. The realtor said that, miraculously, the owner's firm had found her a home in New York City several weeks earlier than they anticipated. The owner also had offered to pay all the closing costs. This was unheard of in that very competitive market. Because a Virginia-specific statute kicked in that weekend that put a lid on the inflation of prices in a year's span, the owner actually reduced the price. I had prayed for the right neighbors, a loving atmosphere, and to meet the needs of the owner. It seemed all these criteria were met.

When all was said and done, we saved an impressive amount of money when the bid wasn't submitted until Monday. The people at the realty firm referred to us as "the people the angels were watching over."

In the next four years, again and again, we realized we had the perfect house, neighbors, and location. The Metro stop was three minutes from our front door and made my commute back to the Pentagon very easy. We also had a beautiful park out the back door, another phenomenal perk in the DC area. In four short years that house sold, yielding a profit large enough to buy our retirement home with cash. This townhouse purchase became our model for understanding we can live "in the house of the Lord forever," and that the Holy Spirit can speak to all people, if only they listen to our Heavenly Father, who has infinitely good ways to bless us.

The qualities are—who you really are!
During a tennis match, a woman on our team fell down and seemed to be losing consciousness. As I held her in my arms, I asked her if I could pray for her until the ambulance arrived. It seemed she was squeezing my hand, meaning OK. I prayed, repeating the Twenty-Third and Ninety-First Psalms that I knew had been a part of her early childhood tradition. The EMS van took her to a nearby hospital.

For several nights I prayed for a sense of peace about the incident. I affirmed it was God who holds our lives in His hands. I recalled the many gracious selfless things she'd done for a neighbor who was a single parent. How lovingly she sent the mom out to shop and take a day off on a regular basis. I didn't stop praying for several nights, until I had established clearly in my thought that her care was in God's hands. It was then I finally felt the needed sense of peace.

At the emergency room they had placed her on life support. As the doctors evaluated her brain injury, they determined it had been so severe that there was no sign of life. They determined they'd take her off life support. However, because her husband was in Europe and they weren't able to contact him, they kept her on the life support. Contrary to what they had assessed, after a few days of being in a deep coma, she unexpectedly took a positive turn. To the shock of the doctors, she recovered and underwent some physical rehabilitation.

Several months later, she showed up at our regular tennis team lesson. It was February and only 22 degrees. She explained that she felt compelled to see me that morning. Although she always had remarked she wasn't religious, she wanted to tell me that the doctors had said there was no human explanation for why she was alive. She told me she and the other team members felt strongly it was because of the prayer on the court. She wanted to thank me. She asked me why I thought she was alive. Then I was appropriately able to share with her some of the ideas I had prayed with. I recounted the qualities she expressed, her kindness, compassion, selflessness, and generosity. I explained I had identified these spiritual qualities as the substance of her life. These qualities she expressed were immortal—they couldn't die. That was who she really was. She seemed uplifted by that explanation and kept affirming that she knew the prayer had been effective.

We played a quick but joyous set of tennis. To see her active, smiling and embracing her newfound value for life was a gift of grace and proof that the Holy Spirit lives in hospital rooms and blesses even when it seems impossible, if a person in prayer is alert to acknowledge God's omnipotence.

The certainty of God's goodness

Returning from a vacation, I realized I was developing a cough. The atmosphere at the Pentagon and in Florida had been one of great fear. People were rehearsing stories of long repetitious stints of a bone-rattling malady. That night I awoke coughing as painfully as I have ever experienced. I naturally turned wholeheartedly to God. One of the proverbs in the Bible was the basis for my response. Proverbs 28:1 establishes the fact that "the righteous are bold as a lion." It came to me to pray boldly.

I sat up and declared what I knew to be true about God. I firmly and sincerely insisted that I did NOT believe that a loving God could ever be responsible for inflicting such a thing on his beloved child. I knew He couldn't have sent it. And that God's goodness included no possibility and certainly no necessity for any such malady. I knew in a moment that the simplicity in Christ's power is that these affirmations of God's love and goodness are the truth. The cough instantaneously disappeared, and that was it.

In these moments of absolute certainty, we stand in awe of God's majesty and power. And it is the great wonder of His grace that heals and is felt as rock solid conviction.

We are one in the Spirit

In February 2004 I received a call from a retired chaplain who was the Seventh Day Adventist endorsing agent for their active duty military chaplains. Both my deputy intelligence command chaplain and I had known this man and his wife for many years and were dearest of friends. He was informing us that he couldn't speak at the Fort Belvoir National Prayer Breakfast. Doctors had discovered his wife had a brain tumor and insisted they must operate immediately. They had explained that such tumors never reduce in size, and they only get bigger quickly.

We asked him if we could pray for her. He said, "Of course!" Then he added they would also pray but that they would be okay with the doctor's efforts if God didn't heal her. Then, after a quiet moment, the tone changed and he seemed to have rethought what he said. He asked me if he understood correctly that I, as a Christian Scientist, would actually be praying for a healing? He asked if he understood that we would believe God would not only be "able" but "willing" to heal this without the surgery. I assured him he understood correctly. I emphasized that it would be a confirmation of the fact that God is that loving and that powerful. He seemed more encouraged and agreed joyously, saying that they also would NOT discount what prayer might accomplish before the scheduled operation.

Both my deputy and my Seventh Day Adventist friends were very devout. Anyone who knew them in the chaplaincy would have described them as "the real deal." They always prayed every day, and their lives were inspiring examples of the teachings of the Bible.

I spent the next two evenings praying. At one point I was acknowledging God's astounding mercy and grandeur. It was a bright moment of absolute conviction. I thought for some time of God as the Great I AM. I felt a sense of peace following this line of thought.

On the third day we received an exultant call from the chaplain endorser alerting us to the fact that the doctors took new pictures for surgery and found the tumor half its original size. Amazed, they recommended not to do anything but watch and to "continue to do whatever it is you're doing." We all again made the commitment to pray vigilantly. I spent time praying again about some specific ideas from *Science and Health with Key to the Scriptures* where Mrs. Eddy points out that "God is the Life, or intelligence, which forms and preserves the individuality and identity of… [humans]" (*Science and Health* 550:5–7). I prayed with the important foundation that God is all and the only cause and only creator of universe, and that "all substance, intelligence, wisdom, being, immortality, cause, and effect belong to God" (*Science and Health* 275:14–15).

At the end of two weeks the doctors re-examined our friend in the hospital. They were astounded to find the tumor completely gone. They stressed they had no medical explanation for what had happened. I know that the prayers of the Seventh Day Adventist couple and my deputy had been sincere conscientious protests of truth. Each of these individuals have been living, loving examples of Christianity and embraced wholeheartedly the commitment we made to do persistent, humble, listening, specific healing prayer for this dear woman we loved. That has been well over ten years ago, and there has been no return of any such symptoms. We were truly one in the Spirit in our prayer.

God only detects the Truth

My stepson was training at the Police Academy. All applicants had to pass a lie detector test. Other officers told him of feeling shame for failing the test and greater fear when having to repeat it. Some candidates had to take it as many as five times to pass it. Non-conclusive tests had to be repeated, and some people never passed it and therefore couldn't be hired. Everyone, including very seasoned officers, said it was the worst experience they'd ever had. The test consisted of four hours of intense interrogation and grilling. It was conducted on the premise that everyone had something they would be tempted to lie about.

He asked me how he might prepare for this excruciating ordeal. I shared with him how I had prayed about having to take two very extensive mandatory physical exams for the military as I closed out my career. It had come to me that there had really been only one examination, and that was when, as in Genesis, "God saw everything he had made, and, behold, it was very good." I offered that he could pause before he entered the room and ask God, Love, to precede him and make easy his way. I reinforced we are never alone. I told him he was a child of God and that was the truth about his identity. I suggested he hold his favorite Bible passage in his thought while he was being tested. He said he would report to me the results.

This is his own description of what happened:

On a crystal clear winter day just before the test, "I was walking the dog and looking at the sky. I was still feeling some concern about the test. At first the suggestion came to me, 'It all hinges on this session.' I was thinking, 'I've done all the things asked of me. I've passed the physical tests, the background checks, and the orals.' It seemed they were putting all their trust in a machine. It seemed incongruous that it would all come down to this arbitrary test. Then I realized I was just thinking of myself. Then I became still enough to listen to God. I recalled the parable about the sparrow (Matthew 10:29–31). I thought, if God's eye is on the sparrow, I'm more important than a sparrow. A machine isn't important to God. I acknowledged that as a child of God I was divinely made. God was reminding me that he wouldn't take me halfway. God assured me, 'It's a man-made instrument, just as imperfect as any machine.'"

During the test, he said, "They made me sit in a room with double-sided windows. It starts with a pre-brief. You sit in a chair that looks like a medieval chair. The intent is to plant a seed of doubt. The interrogator said, 'You can't beat the machine.' For twenty minutes he explained that any hesitation or halfway response, once I was hooked up, would be identified. He repeated it didn't matter how disciplined I was. He said he knew I was an athlete, but the machine can pick up the slightest nuance and the subtlest variance. I was still for two hours. I sat so still there was no sensation in my legs. For two hours they read me the questions and recorded my responses.

"The second two hours they hooked me up to the lie detector machine and compared my responses. I pictured the Twenty-Third Psalm as if it were a picture book. I kept thinking about what it meant. I recall especially being comforted by the words 'He maketh me to lie down in green pastures…He restoreth my soul.' And another Bible assurance, from Isaiah 26, 'Thou wilt keep him in perfect peace, whose mind is stayed on thee' comforted my heart. I also went back to the peace and calm I'd felt looking at that still starry sky.

"During the session I noticed the interrogator kept repositioning the sensors, fiddling with the machine, and even turned it off and on. At one point the tester put the sensors on himself. I felt peaceful and just focused on the psalm. When the test was over, the officer asked if I would speak to him outside the office. I asked if I'd passed the test, and the officer said yes. When I joined him in the hall, the man peered into my eyes and asked in an amazed manner, 'Who are you?' I thought, gee! We just spent four hours discussing that. I asked him, 'Didn't I cover that in the questioning?' The man looked seriously, again, deep into my eyes and said, 'No! WHO ARE YOU?' even more emphatically. I had to ask him to explain. The officer told me he'd been a detective and state policeman for fifteen years. He had given lie detector tests for years to literally hundreds of people, and he'd never, ever had a test come out like that. He exclaimed, 'It was like I was hooked up to a dead man! You had no readings!' The man just shook his head and assured me he had tested and retested the machine to assure himself that it was working. It had worked fine on him. Then I explained that I had prayed, and he just shook his head.

"I had initially been scheduled to take the test in March but the date was moved up to February. That meant I was hired within three weeks of starting the initial application. I called my stepmother [that was me] afterward very triumphant and told her that I felt only peace and calm during the entire test. I asked if she had any idea what had happened. She told me, as best she could explain, that I had grasped that I wasn't a mortal to be read and examined, but one of God's sheep who followed and obeyed the Lord as his shepherd. Having held in my consciousness that I was God's child, and that was my identity, it couldn't be read on a lie detector machine."

He had met the machine—and mastered it.

Experiences like I had move the heart, unite people, and make them more aware of the holiness of all life. At those times we forgive, we repent, or we grow in our sense of love for God and mankind. These were all by-products of the great spiritual growth a woman chaplain or any religious professional would experience throughout a career in the ministry. We were seeing that civilian women in occupations on the home front were making their way and were experiencing some of the same healings, finding progress, as we did. These were all indicators we were on the right track.

CHAPTER 8
THE STEEL AND THE VELVET OF CHARACTER

...thy rod and thy staff they comfort me.
"Mercy and truth are met together..." (Psalm 85)

In my twenty-eight years of service, I often felt I was learning what good leadership looked like. Other times I saw leadership mistakes I'd want to avoid. Through my many unusual experiences, I came to the conclusion that leadership is an art.

When people discuss leadership, it isn't uncommon to consider two quite different techniques that inform how a leader proceeds in any given situation. Sometimes the issues are moral, legal, or safety issues, and there is no yielding. At those times the leader must show the "steel" in character to do the right thing. I've always likened that to the shepherd's use of the "rod" in the scriptures.

At other times it's appropriate to show empathy or compassion, or just to take a much more indirect path that isn't openly challenging. These are the "velvet" traits of character. That is what I'd liken to the staff of the loving shepherd. It gently guides the lamb into the fold.

In some situations you see a combination of the two. Often, the art of leadership is to orchestrate just the right combination of the two elements. In my experience as a chaplain, it was when people pressed the moral envelope that I leaned toward the side of the steel. In a male hierarchical organization such as the military, you ran into a lot of people whose dominant inclination was the steel mode. Then chaplains sometimes were able to temper the course ahead by reminding the leaders that both types of leadership can be appropriate.

Forceful utterances? Only when appropriate

In 1977 as a new captain at Fort Sill, I was told to report to the Artillery Training Center (ATC) commander, a colonel, who was three ranks above me. He promptly put me at a position of attention in front of his desk. I noticed he had left the door open, and his secretary's desk was right by the entrance to his office. He demanded in a very gruff tone, "Why aren't you at home having some man's babies?" It seemed apparent that he wanted to shock or bully me.

I stood very quietly for a moment to let him feel the impact of the silence. He had spoken so loudly his secretary had taken offense at what he said. She got up and stood in the doorway, looking so angry I thought her hair might catch fire. This was a moment I would think back on many times in the future. It would have been hard to imagine too many other statements a man could have said to a woman that would have been more offensive.

I knew this would be a pivotal moment. I prayed and listened. It came to me that he needed to hear the absolutely last answer he would've expected. Very softly and yet with a depth of emotion, I said, "What if I told you that I couldn't have children?" You could see the shock in his facial expression. His demeanor changed. He looked very embarrassed. After a very quiet, painful moment, I said, "What if I told you that I was so grateful for the life God gave me, that I decided to dedicate it to ministering to soldiers rather than lying around feeling sorry for myself?" He slid down in his chair, even more embarrassed. He quietly dismissed me and told me I should report to my unit. As I left, his secretary met my eyes and seemed to smile in appreciation as a show of support.

During that year and a half, the colonel struck terror in nearly everyone's heart other than mine. On two other occasions, I found that he needed to hear things he wasn't expecting to hear. In my first year I designed a workshop in which we finally convinced the commander to build in break time between training cycles for our greatly overworked drill sergeants. At his request I also captained a women's team for the ATC in our installation's track meet.

When I was due to rotate to Korea for a new assignment, the colonel called me to his office. He wanted me to know that he had personally written on my final evaluation. This is unheard of, and it required a Department of the Army-level exception to policy. In the seven years I worked personnel policy at the Pentagon, I never saw it done again in any of the 1,500-plus records I reviewed. As a leader two ranks above my boss, he was only supposed to review my evaluation. He had added a separate document to the evaluation form and wanted to read it to me himself. Much to my surprise, it stated that in his career he had never encountered such a natural and insightful leader. It was a glowing report that remained in my permanent record.

After he read me the evaluation, he insisted he needed to personally apologize to me for what he'd said the first day. I kept insisting he didn't need to. Finally, I said firmly, "No, sir, you don't need to apologize!" Exasperated, he asked me, "Why not?" And I said, "Because all I said to you was, 'What if…?'" I explained that by the army's personnel policy women weren't allowed to have children, so technically what I had said was true by their design. He broke into a smile and said, "Well, I guess I deserved that, too!" I heard his secretary giggling. I turned to see she had positioned herself in the doorway to hear the apology. I saluted him and shook his hand.

God's way of teaching may take some unusual forms that we could never design. I have come to know it will include a power that is both meek and strongly divine.

It's only justice if it's joined with mercy

In 1982 two colonels barged into my office. One was our installation chaplain, and the other was our supervisory chaplain for the chapel at Fort Ord, California. They informed me that they were bringing charges against one of our chaplain assistants for taking money from the chapel offerings. I knew the young man was having financial difficulties and had helped him one month. He had returned the small loan promptly.

The installation chaplain was red in the face and full of righteous indignation. He blustered at me, "I want blood!" I sat quietly affirming that God never made a thief. It came to me to ask him if it was okay if all I wanted was justice. That took some of the wind out of his sails. He did explain that an audit showed the assistant had taken money several times but replaced all but a very small amount of the money.

As I prayed, it came to me that the punishment should not exceed the crime. I realized army regulation directed that the battalion commander would determine the chaplain assistant's discipline. The commander wisely chose only non-judicial punishment because it was the young private's first offense. The chaplain assistant asked me to represent him at the hearing that would determine the specifics of his punishment. The words of Psalm 119 seemed to pinpoint the purpose I would have in this matter: "Plead my cause, and deliver me…Thy word is true from the beginning: and every one of thy righteous judgments endureth for ever." The psalm had taught me from my youth that I could be assured that judgment was really in God's hands, not men's. I knew God would help me know what to say.

In the hearing I pointed out that the assistant was really being doubly punished, since his pending promotion to specialist was canceled and the commander was reducing him from his current grade of private first class (PFC/E-3) to a private (PVT/E-2). I also asked the commander to consider the fact that the young man already had financial problems, so extra duty rather than a fine might be a more compassionate punishment. The commander agreed and ruled in a very fair manner.

After the young soldier left the office, the commander remarked to me that he thought I had missed my calling. He suggested I could have been a great attorney. We both thanked God that the commander had shown such wisdom and mercy in the entire matter.

Honesty wins a tennis match with the guys

In 1982, when I was at the Defense Language Institute Chapel at the Presidio, some marines taught me to play what they called "power tennis." After that I often comically referred to my tennis style as "Kamikaze" tennis.

Some of the guys I worked with asked me to play on their summer tennis team. I was the only woman on the team. The total number of games won determined which team won the overall match. In my singles match, I was absolutely shocked when the guy I played against called every ball out that came anywhere near a line. I began to try to win points by shots that were so clearly in, even he couldn't call them out. However, he continued to call some points out that landed as much as a foot inside the line.

I wanted to see something better, higher, and holier in the day. So I began to pray about it. The idea came to me that it wasn't up to him or me to decide the match. That encouraged me so much, I asked God not to let the match ride on the outcome of our games. I was extremely grateful when the final score was exactly five games each. That nullified any influence our match could have in determining the winner.

Much to my surprise, the man I played was chosen to play in the deciding doubles match. I had told my teammates that I didn't really play doubles and that two of the guys should play the final. They begged me to play. They felt I was one of the top two players, and the match would ride on the outcome of that final doubles match.

I gave in and began the match. The young man continued to call out many of the balls I hit that were well in the court. I quickly began to declare that God was good and He was present with us. I again asked Him not to let me be any part of determining the outcome. At this point, the men on the opposing team who were watching began to correct the unfair calls. Even the man's double's partner began to correct the unfair calls on my shots.

Our team didn't have to do anything other than play our best tennis. The guy who continued to relentlessly call my shots out got angrier and angrier as his teammates corrected call after call. We won the match by a couple of games.

Afterward, my teammates were still incensed that someone could be that unfair and dishonest. They kept insisting the man was only calling my shots out because I was a woman. Another teammate added it wasn't just because I was a woman. He felt the guy called them out because a woman was beating him. All I knew was the fact that honesty triumphed over dishonesty. God's ever-present goodness is always discernible in our day and, in some cases, our play.

A salute to a Vietnam veteran at the VFW

In 1986 my boss at the Combined Arms Department (CAD) invited all the staff to join him at the local Veterans of Foreign Wars (VFW) club. He always made time to attend the annual meal prepared for disabled veterans from a nearby assisted living home. It was rare that any of us would miss the opportunity to chat with and encourage the men on these occasions.

One evening as we sat around the table, I was very engrossed in talking with a man who was a veteran of World War II. I vaguely remember my boss, a lieutenant colonel, asking me to point at numbers on a piece of paper he kept shoving my way. I really didn't have a clue why he kept pushing the paper in front of me. I humored him because I didn't want to interrupt the man's story of his unit's participation in some pretty famous battles. Towards the end of the evening, the nurses came to take the veterans back to their care center.

When I turned back toward the CAD team, the lieutenant colonel

(LTC) told me that almost every number I pointed to had been a winning number in the drawings that were held. I looked to see the table was now filled with numerous gifts. One in particular was in a pretty wooden box. The LTC said it wasn't something he'd want and that I should take it. Because all the items were for men, he suggested I give it away. I noticed a man with a hat on at the bar. It was a ball cap with the words "Vietnam Veteran" on it. In the early to mid-1980s Vietnam vets didn't usually wear identifying clothing items.

The man seemed to be unusually quiet and seemed very much alone. For those reasons I took the box and walked up to him. I showed him the contents and asked if he'd like to have it. He smiled and happily said, "Sure!" He asked me why I wanted to give it to him. I pointed at his hat and said, "I would give it to you for that." Much to my surprise, he seemed offended and took the hat off and clutched it close to his chest. He said, "No, thanks. I would never give this hat away for anything." I realized he thought I wanted to trade the gift for the hat. I quietly explained that wasn't what I meant. I told him I would like to give it to him as a thank-you for his service. You could see extreme shock in his face as he broke into tears. He grabbed me and gave me a very warm and genuine hug as he continued to weep. He finally gathered himself. He told me that was the first time anyone had ever thanked him or even said anything nice to him about his service.

When I returned to the CAD table, they were all a bit teary-eyed, also. They were serious for a few moments and then threw themselves into ribbing me about making the soldier cry. It's so different today. I can see how much progress has been made in adopting a much healthier and decent attitude toward all the men and women who choose to serve in the military. And gentleness is always a good quality at times when someone can benefit from appreciation and comfort.

"Mercy and truth are met together…"

While I was serving in Indianapolis at Fort Benjamin Harrison in the 1980s, a very bright student in one of my basic course ethics classes seemed to delight in raising his hand to answer every question in our discussions. The young lieutenant always knew the material flawlessly and never missed class. It was evident in the other students' looks and nods to each other that they considered him what they called a "know-it-all."

One day he came in looking very despondent. Then I realized he had a rather dark-looking black and blue bruise on his face. After class I asked him what had happened. He shrugged it off, saying that the other students didn't appreciate him.

The next class I gave him a card with a quote on it from Mary Baker Eddy: "Your advancing course may provoke envy, but it will also attract respect" (*Science and Health* 452:11–12). I told him that I did appreciate the stellar intelligence he expressed. I assured him he was not only appreciated by the instructors, but even more importantly by God, for valuing the intelligence He had given him. I let him know I had struggled with shyness and embarrassment about being considered "the smart girl" in my early teens.

I explained that like a star that shines very brightly, it can seem like it draws attention away from the things around it that don't shine so brightly. I suggested he could understand that it would be gracious on his part to allow some of the other students to volunteer answers, also. I encouraged him to join his love for knowledge with the leadership quality of humility and the Christian virtues of grace and mercy referred to in Psalm 85. I emphasized that he could understand that really stellar intelligence does provoke envy, but that senior leaders would value and respect the wisdom he could bring to a military team or staff.

It was good to see his normal smile return to his face. It was even better to see he did heed the wisdom of the Word and began to be a bit more understated in his manner. It was a blessing for everyone when he adopted a manner that was in tune with the timeless wisdom of the Psalm, a gentle and velvet glove that also seemed to be the right step for comforting him.

Pretty in pink

When I left the Pentagon in 1993 after my first assignment there, the army chief of chaplains personally pinned on my tour award. I thought it would be a very typical ceremony. However, very few things in my career were ever typical. My male counterparts were going to make sure it was a day I'd remember.

My boss, the director of personnel, wanted to indelibly etch this day in my memory, so he gathered the personnel team just prior to the ceremony. They had painted a Kevlar helmet pink and affixed pretty pink gift-wrapping bows on the edges encircling the entire steel pot/helmet.

The colonel's wife had taken an olive drab pistol belt and tied individual pink ribbons through all the little eyelets on the belt. A disarmed pink hand grenade completed the striking array.

If all the pink wasn't eye-catching enough, the guys drew even more attention as they sang a Jody call created especially for me. They loudly chanted, "Sing it loud and sing it clearly, don't you call my chaplain 'Dearie'!"

You'd probably think that was about the end of it. But I didn't realize until I was attempting to exit the building what distress this caused for the security guards. Somehow they weren't really comfortable with my carrying a hand grenade in the corridors of the Pentagon—even if it was painted pink. Gratefully, many of them knew me because I baked them pies and cookies when they had to work on the holidays.

To this day, whenever anyone sees these items in my office, they stop, smile, and say, "There's got to be a story to this!" Well, it was just another one of the many fond memories of my tenure in the five-sided building. And it was also a very fitting finishing touch to another segment of the journey for a woman officer and chaplain.

Bearing true witness in a matrix of beliefs

When I arrived in Germany, there was a chaplain working for me who came from a very conservative tradition. I noticed he had a matrix posted on his door that depicted the beliefs of about twenty Christian faith groups. I read the column that supposedly represented my denominational beliefs. I mentioned to him that the matrix didn't accurately depict our concepts. He just shrugged it off and said nothing. Our Catholic priest at the area support group chapel was in the office, and I asked him to review the column labeled Roman Catholic. He also remarked to the chaplain the matrix was incorrect for his church.

I told him our church would gladly fill in an identical matrix of categories for him that would correctly represent our beliefs. Father agreed his church would be more than willing to do the same. Because the chaplain with the matrix didn't respond to our offer in any way, I also offered him an insight. I mentioned that, for me, it was a matter of not bearing "false witness against [your] neighbor." I assured him my experience with him in those first few weeks had convinced me he was an honest man. He asked me if I was directing him to take it down. I told him that was not the case. I emphasized that it had to be his decision.

I also asked him if he was aware our black chaplain assistants wouldn't enter his office because of a Confederate flag he had displayed in a presentation plaque. I noted that was why they would only hand items in to him at the door of his office. They would come to my office by a back door so they wouldn't have to pass by it to talk to me. He looked surprised and said he wasn't aware of that. The issue of the Confederate flag was a very fiery cultural issue at that time. I asked him if he realized that there might be soldiers who wouldn't come to him for counseling if this were an issue to them. He quietly listened, and I could tell he was beginning to think about what we discussed.

I never said another word to him about either issue. I immediately began to pray to acknowledge he could hear God's direction and that nothing could separate us from God's love for all His people. I committed myself to seeing his God-given strengths. Over time I saw he was a man of great spiritual strength and commitment. He was a talented preacher and reunited our chapel community when a controversy could have torn it apart.

In about two weeks he voluntarily took down the matrix and took the picture with the flag to his home. Our friendship became very genuine over the year we served together. He repeatedly showed what a man of stellar moral character he was, and I rejoiced to support him in prayer through two very trying experiences. It wasn't necessary at all to "get tough" to find right results in this receptive heart.

Having the record vs. equitable assignment opportunity

In 1994 I was astonished when I was called into the commanding general's office toward the end of my tour in Germany and informed I had been selected as the first woman chaplain to attend the army's senior service college at Carlisle Barracks, Pennsylvania. That school selection normally signals your competitiveness for the highest-level promotions and assignments in your branch of service.

Shortly after I arrived in Carlisle, I was quite taken aback when the male chaplain who was an instructor on the faculty of the Army War College suddenly volunteered that he'd been on the board that selected me for the school. He told me that he wanted me to know that I actually did have the kind of stellar record that deserved to be chosen for the resident course. I knew he was attempting to compliment me. But I didn't know what to say. I just smiled and was silent.

Then he realized that what he said could imply that he hadn't thought that would be the case. He blushed slightly and began to backpedal a bit. He told me that most people would assume that the board had been forced to make an equal opportunity selection, and I was the first woman chaplain to qualify to be in the zone for consideration. He underscored that it was truly rare that a junior lieutenant colonel was selected.

He also noted that not all the male selections were based on the quality of the chaplain's record. He noted that some were based on an advocate on the board or, in our branch, which denominations were most competitive for future selection as an army chief of chaplains. He told me that my male peers would receive competitive assignments following their attendance. That was indeed the case with almost all the chaplains who attended. However, it wasn't the case for me. He mentioned later that he couldn't figure out whether that was because of gender bias or prevalent misunderstandings about my denomination. That would be a question that would be the subject of much debate over the coming years.

Once again, taking the front rank had put me in a position of much scrutiny. In my next assignment at the chaplain school, I often heard rumors or got emails that implied I had only received the War College slot as an equal opportunity gift that was forced on the army chief of chaplains office. Most people didn't realize these selection boards were closely scrutinized by the Department of the Army Secretariat and were run by army competitive officers and that even the majority of voting members were not chaplains. Fair and square is part of the moral undergirding of the best of army life.

My Name is Nikita Khrushchev

One of the required exercises at the Army War College was a debate designed to see if you could argue a position that you didn't agree with. Our international officer from the Czech Republic and I were asked in 1995 to argue a position that the United States started the Cold War. Our army judge and another senior colonel were to argue that the USSR started the Cold War. We were given documents that included points to support the different positions.

Because English was our Czech officer's second language, he asked to write out and read his argument. He did so very deliberately and finished quietly. Both persons on the particular side of an issue were supposed to finish before the other team started their opposing arguments. Before I could begin my oral presentation, our judge prematurely started to attack our Czech officer's arguments. I could see Ivo was visibly shaken and even a bit embarrassed. He was at a disadvantage trying to translate everything being said.

Even before I realized what I was doing, a flash of protectiveness came over me. It was as if I went into character and played the scene as if two homegrown Soviets were being accused of starting the Cold War. I took off my shoe and slammed it down on the table in imitation of Khrushchev in the United Nations. And much to even my surprise, I launched into an impassioned argument that the US had started the Cold War. For some reason I found I was speaking with a convincing Russian accent. I stood bombarding the judge and his partner with bullet after bullet of reasons. They flew out of my mouth like they were emotional and strong convictions on my part. I never looked at a note or paused to think.

Ivo's eyes were wide, and he had a completely shocked look on his face. When I finished there was a brief period of silence. Then the judge spoke. He said, "Darn, chaplain, if I didn't know better, I'd be convinced the US started the Cold War!" Everyone burst into laughter, and Ivo just stared at me in disbelief.

Shortly after that, he and the Jordanian brigadier general asked if I would teach them tennis. We were fast friends after that. There were so many priceless experiences during that year. We had a great class, and we all grew to understand the varied perspectives among the branch specialties. Our foreign officers added a dimension that was as rich an insight as the entire course curriculum. I mark that school as one of my favorite years in my twenty-eight-year army career and also a story from my "tough" or steely side.

Listening as the Father would

A classmate in my seminar at the Army War College that year was concerned about his changing relationship with his teenage daughter. He remarked he thought he was losing her. I could see the agony in his face.

I asked if he were willing to try something. He said, "Yes," and I recommended he go home and ask his daughter to talk. But I cautioned him that to be effective, he had to promise not to talk himself for at least fifteen minutes. To emphasize how difficult it might be, I gave him guidelines. I explained if he had to sit on his hands or put duct tape over his mouth—he must do whatever was necessary. I encouraged him that if he could listen for even longer, he should do it. I clarified that it would be okay to nod and acknowledge he was listening—but there would be no words on his part.

He came back the next day beaming. He rejoiced that he had listened for over an hour. At that point, his daughter stopped talking and threw her arms around him. He told me in a deeply moving tone that she beamed and said, "Daddy, that's the first time you've listened to me in years."

He had engaged not just physical ears. Truly listening is not merely a matter of having functioning flaps of skin hanging on the side of your face. He had humbly engaged his heart. It had a profound healing effect on the relationship. He agreed his experience should be shared if it could help anyone.

By the numbers—A Muslim chaplain for the V Corps

In 1999 as the V Corps Chaplain in Heidelberg, Germany, I got a call from the European Command personnel office informing me that a battalion commander had refused his programmed chaplain replacement. The battalion chaplain had convinced both the battalion and brigade commanders that the soldiers would never accept a Muslim chaplain. This prompted the brigade commander, a colonel, to call the chaplain personnel officer and back up the battalion's refusal of the assignment of the Muslim chaplain.

When he called me, I directed the personnel chaplain to tell the brigade commander my exact response by the numbers. I told him to be very sure that he never used the word "no" in the discussion. I explained that commanders tend to have very well developed egos, and that he did not want to come off as insubordinate in any way. However, we were going to tell the colonel "no" without using that word.

I told the personnel chaplain to start by emphasizing that the corps chaplain wanted to protect him. He would then walk him through the steps needed to decline the Muslim chaplain. First, the personnel chaplain would explain that he needed to put in writing that he was declining the Muslim chaplain and why, and he was to sign and date that document. As the corps chaplain, I would then advise him to run the document by an attorney and to take it to the equal opportunity officer for the division. He would be wise to have them review the regulations and legal implications of his decision.

I also recommended that the commander should discuss the declination with the division chaplain because I didn't think his own departing battalion chaplain had advised him wisely in this matter. I informed him the three-star general, the corps commander, had been very excited at the prospect of having a Muslim chaplain available to advise us on Muslim issues in our numerous Balkan task forces. I told him to explain that he would probably be waiting at least six months to a year before he would get the next replacement chaplain. He would need to coordinate indirect chaplain coverage with the division chaplain. I instructed him to close by emphasizing that all of these steps would serve to protect him from making a decision that might have any negative backlash for his career.

There was a long pause when I finished, and then the personnel chaplain said, "Well, that ought to do it." It wasn't long after that I received a second call telling me that both the brigade and battalion commanders had decided to accept the Muslim chaplain.

A couple of weeks later, I got a call from the battalion commander, saying he was very happy with the new chaplain. He had seen the chaplain complete the longer training runs with the troops and realized that they all seemed inspired by him. He mentioned they had found the man had been a Christian before he had converted to Islam, and therefore he knew both faith groups' belief systems well.

About two months later, I was at the three-star general's corps training conference for all his subordinate commanders. A brigade commander, a colonel, I had never met before walked up to me and was visibly reading my nametag and obviously checking out the chaplain cross on my uniform. He introduced himself as the brigade commander who "owned the Muslim chaplain." We shook hands, and he said he was happy to finally meet me. He wanted to thank me for taking care of him and his subordinate battalion commander when the Muslim chaplain issue had been discussed. Then he smiled and exclaimed, "Gee! I thought you'd be bigger!" I took that as a confirmation that when you speak the truth, its authority is always felt as larger than fear or human biases. Truth has its own strong and permanent strength.

CHAPTER 9
LOVE OVERCOMING HATE

Thou preparest a table before me in the presence of mine enemies:

When I went to the Pentagon in 2000 as executive director of the Armed Forces Chaplain Board, it was one of the high points of my career. I could review my years as a military chaplain to date as I entered this watershed moment. It was increasingly clear with each day that this ministry was a rewarding calling. On many a day you saw how powerfully the Word of the scriptures quieted fear or comforted a troubled heart. Many who saw the sincerity of our chaplains joined forces to support them. In my case, when biases reared their head, just by my being a friend and achieving a mission, the bonds grew stronger every hour among those of us serving, and many displayed the best in human character.

Reviewing my military life up to that point caused me to think of the steps I (and the others) took as we served as women chaplains in a new and challenging time. I asked myself what was the greatest tool I had to move the situation forward and experience progress, and the answer was clear. Love, for God and man, is the greatest tool. As I returned to the Pentagon, I would need these tools, and "the greatest of these is love," as the Apostle Paul states.

Abraham Lincoln was once asked what he was going to do to get rid of a man in his cabinet who seemed to be his enemy. He answered that he would love the man until he was his friend, and then he would have gotten rid of his enemy. "Simply count your enemy to be that which defiles, defaces, and dethrones the Christ-image that you should reflect. Whatever purifies, sanctifies, and consecrates human life, is not an enemy, however much we suffer in the process" (*Miscellaneous Writings*

1893–1896, 8:17–21).

In the first years, as we have shown in the earlier chapters, it was harder for some people to accept that women were serving as military chaplains. Sometimes the way people reacted was quite negative. I relied heavily on the scriptures to help neutralize hateful responses.

These experiences reminded me of how Moses had to turn aside and see how a bush could burn but not be consumed before he could have the endurance to road-march people for forty years through the desert. When I took a healing approach to being met with hatred, it often turned the situation around. It became the very experience that heightened my patience, and I felt more capable of following in the Master's footsteps. I'll trace these times when "love won" through my years in the military.

The antagonistic radio personality

The time was 1976, the place Fort Sill, Oklahoma. While I was unpacking, the phone rang. A radio personality asked if I was Chaplain Janet Yarlott. This show was live, and I didn't know it. Ethically, he should have told me I was on the radio.

"How can you call yourself a minister and serve with the baby killers in the military?" he demanded. The press in that day had no love affair with the military because of the Vietnam War. I paused a moment and prayed silently for God's help. Despite his hateful bearing, I thought an answer of peace was truly what was needed. It came to me to tell him what I had observed.

I told him that I had been in the military less than one week. Yet, in that short time it didn't seem that the soldiers were any different than people I had met anywhere else. Granted, they weren't pampered rich people or ivory tower scholars but largely people from modest backgrounds. And it was apparent to me that the military was certainly the largest equal opportunity employer in the United States. "The soldiers I have met had the same hopes, the same loves, the same fears and the same goals as any of the humble people I had met in the Midwest where I grew up," I said. "They seem to me to be largely people who just want an opportunity to feed their families and have a chance to get started in life."

This was obviously not the answer he was expecting. There was a moment of dead air, and then he hung up on me. I remember thanking

God for that outcome.

The next day at work I was called to the commanding general's office. He told me that his public affairs officer (PAO) had briefed him on my radio interview. I explained the radio host hadn't told me we were on the air. The general was pleased with my warm and genuine response. He was even more excited about the positive response by people in the Lawton area. He congratulated me and let me know that if I got other calls I could direct the media to his PAO. He reiterated they weren't supposed to call me directly. He remarked that I seemed to be wise beyond my years. "I've relied on my PAO, my heavenly Father, for that answer," I said. He smiled a very dear smile and told me I could do any coverage as far as he was concerned. "Keep on praying," he told me as I left.

Playing on the volleyball team: The many vs. the one

When our infantry battalion played in the Fort Sill volleyball league, the men invited me to join the team. During the warm-up for the first game, the other team made some disparaging remarks about the stupidity of allowing a woman to play. The captain of the infantry team made it clear that if it was all right with them—it should be all right with the other team.

The very first time a ball came over the net by me, I leaped in the air and spiked it for a winner. This caused the men in their front row some consternation. The next time their server hit the ball over the net toward my position, I went up for the ball. When I attempted to block the ball, a guy from the other team came completely under the net and knocked my legs out from under me in mid-air. I hit the floor pretty hard. As I was gathering myself, these words from the 91st Psalm came to me, "For he shall give his angels charge over thee, to keep thee in all thy ways. They shall bear thee up in their hands, lest thou dash thy foot against a stone." I completely trusted God to remove the "stone" from the men's hearts. I picked myself up and got back in position for the next point.

What followed was a bit extraordinary. The referee for the match looked astonished. He immediately red-carded the man. The ejected artilleryman stood there rather defiant and thought his team would support him. But I must credit all the other men on the floor that night. Not one of the other men in the gymnasium, including his own teammates, supported his vehement protest. They made it clear he was no longer a part of the artillery team. I was so grateful to see that the goodness of the many far outweighed the malice of the one.

Not just the easy footsteps

Having been spat on three times, I've always said the first time is the hardest. You learn a lot in these types of intense challenges. When I was at the US Army Chaplain School in 1980, a chaplain confronted me when he saw the unusually high-level awards I had on my uniform for someone very new in the military. He made a disparaging remark about women being chaplains and insisted I couldn't possibly have deserved the two meritorious service medals. Shockingly, he spat on me. My reaction was a lot like someone igniting a gas grill. I was white hot with anger because it felt so demeaning. I turned all my attention to God to attempt to understand what had just happened. Instantaneous self-awareness of what is happening in your own thought is critical. I knew if I didn't get my "self" in hand, I would probably regret what I might be capable of doing.

That immediate and momentary turning away from the human situation turned my thought to Mary Baker Eddy's counsels in our denominational textbook: "You must control evil thoughts in the first instance, or they will control you in the second" (*Science and Health* 234:26–27). I thought of this in a slightly different sense. I knew I must control my thought in that first instant. That's how alert I needed to be in this base situation.

I now realized this was a matter of purifying my own heart. It was as if I were getting a stern and poignant counseling session from the Lord. What I heard in my thought was, "The soldiers spat on Jesus." That spiritual insight alone floored me, and I felt humbled in the greatest sense. Then the rebuke continued, "When you said you wanted to follow me, did you think I meant only in the easy footsteps?" I responded, "No, Lord, I will follow you all the way to the cross if that is what's necessary!" Instantaneously, any semblance of anger was quenched and another thought came: "What must a person have been through in order to be able to bring himself to spit on another human being?"

My response absolutely reversed itself. I felt a deep sense of compassion and pity. I reached out and embraced him. I repeated what I'd heard and said I couldn't imagine what he must have been through if he could spit on another human being. The recognition of what he had done in a moment of anger seemed to hit him like a brick in the face. He fell to his knees and begged me to forgive him. I told him I certainly would.

Later in my career someone asked me who spat on me. The man who had done that was another student in a very large Chaplain Officer Advanced Course, and I hadn't met him before that day in 1981. I had no desire to attach the event to him personally. I wanted to remember who he really was—a child of God. I have ceased to associate the incident with a person, and I see no face in my memory at all. I think that was the most important part of the healing.

The Bible account of Shadrach, Meshach, and Abednego assures us the fire doesn't have to have any power over us—just the reverse is true: "Blessed are they which are persecuted for righteousness' sake: for theirs is the kingdom of heaven" (Matthew 5:10). When we face challenges, we shouldn't be discouraged, because they can deeply bless us. But we must demand our blessing as Jacob did at Peniel and continue to wrestle with their lessons until we understand them. Trials are a part of the path of spiritual progress. By giving earnest heed to these spiritual guides, as the book of Hebrews (13:2) describes, we "entertain angels unawares."

"Blessed are the peacemakers"

Late in my first tour at the Pentagon in the chief of chaplains office in 1989, I came to realize that although I was grateful to be there, it still had its challenges. In 1991 a new assignments officer arrived. Shortly after joining the office, he made openly racist remarks, and he quickly made it known he didn't like me either. That surprised me because he and I had been in the same Chaplain Officer Basic Course. I hadn't recalled his being that way before. He seemed to have changed greatly as he had advanced in rank.

One morning as I was riding the Metro to work, I attempted to read my weekly Bible lesson. Oddly, it was as if a voice in my consciousness were urging me loudly and repeatedly to acknowledge a biblical truth from the Beatitudes: "Blessed are the peacemakers! Blessed are the peacemakers!" It was so dominant I couldn't hear anything else. I yielded to this direction and turned obediently to the Sermon on the Mount and studied it for the remainder of my ride to the Pentagon.

I didn't know at that time that the new chaplain assignments officer would be in a meeting that afternoon or that the meeting would address an issue emotional to him. It was clear to me later that God knew! The meeting included my boss, his replacement, and our executive officer, as well as the assignments officer and me. The director of personnel had received calls from chaplains who had completed degree programs for specific instructor slots at service schools that this assignments officer had assigned to unrelated jobs. Something was not right. When we attempted to find out why, he began to call me a "filthy liar." His attacks only intensified when it became clear he placed personal friends with no training for the instructor jobs in the pre-assigned slots—simply because it was a geographical location his friends wanted.

It was striking that the angrier the man got, the more compassion and pity I felt for him. I was compelled by the idea of the beatitude that the peacemakers are indeed blessed. I even found myself explaining his possible misperceptions on the issue in support of him. I told him as the assignments officer he could change any chaplain and his family's life with the stroke of a pen. For that reason they might feel reluctant to be candid with him when he sent them to assignments that didn't utilize the degrees they had so diligently completed. He became so irate that he called me an extremely derogatory name and stormed out of the office in a rage, nearly charging into another action officer as he entered the hallway. The meeting came to an abrupt end.

My new chaplain personnel boss was a graduate of West Point and a former combat arms officer. He was the only chaplain in the meeting who seemed to admit anything inappropriate had happened. He asked me to step outside by the heliport. He told me that in all of his years as a cadet, as a combat arms officer, and now a chaplain of twenty years, he had never seen anyone exercise the kind of loving self-control I did in that meeting. Later another chaplain action officer said he thought the assignments chaplain looked so angry that it appeared he'd explode. "Yet when I saw you, I realized I'd never seen anyone look so peaceful and calm as you did when you left the meeting."

Over the next few days, the man's attacks continued, even drawing the attention of many of the attorneys who worked with us on legal issues. About that time anonymous letters arrived for our generals, the army chief of chaplains and his deputy. The executive officer, a chaplain who was a colonel, called me in and told me he had opened both letters. He was a friend and protector of the younger assignments officer. "I just want you to know the letters are out there," he said. In these two identical letters the writer called me a "filthy liar" and the exact derogatory name as in the meeting. They were postmarked in Alexandria, where that assignments officer lived, and they were dated the day after the meeting. The executive officer told me he was certain the letters weren't from the assignments chaplain who had demeaned me. I asked him how anyone else would have known the exact wording he had used. He didn't respond to my question.

I went directly to the Judge Advocate General's office and talked to the attorneys I knew. They were appalled that nothing had been done. They were intent on convincing me he should be charged with conduct unbecoming an officer, verbal assault, and equal opportunity complaints. They seemed dismayed that the three chaplain colonels in the meeting had not stepped in or provided any leadership immediately when the abuse started. For my part, however, I had to reconsider whether we should proceed with legal action. I explained that I had never seen litigation significantly change people's biases. I also didn't want to risk reprisals negatively influencing my next assignment or my career. I felt I needed to continue to apply the beatitude, and I prayed to be the peacemaker. Peacemaking doesn't really come from suing anyone. However, one of the attorneys insisted I get the letters and allow them to review the content.

When I returned to the chief of chaplains office about an hour later, the executive officer stepped into the doorway and blocked me from entering the office where he had thrown the letter into the general's wastebasket earlier that afternoon. He nervously insisted it wasn't in there because the cleaning lady took the trash. I told him that I had worked in the office for nearly four years and the cleaning lady came about nine o'clock every morning. He forcefully asserted it was gone. I asked him for the second letter that had been addressed to the brigadier general who was our deputy. He again insisted that it was gone. "Are you in the habit of opening the mail of others?" I wanted to know. He simply wouldn't answer. When I updated the attorneys, they just shook their heads and asked, "Isn't it the chaplains who are supposed to be the guardians of ethical standards?" I told them that the chief of chaplains was on the road, and the deputy had been out of the office when it happened. This was more about the executive officer protecting his friend.

When the chief of chaplains returned, I told him about the name calling in the original meeting and the letters. I suggested that he should be able to assure every person who worked in our offices that such public attacks wouldn't be tolerated. I underlined that I had faith in his leadership. "What do you think would be appropriate?" he wanted to know. I answered directly: "The assignments officer should have to apologize in front of the same people he had demeaned me in front of." He agreed and convened a meeting in his office the next morning.

The assignments officer entered the office and still seemed so angry that he could barely contain himself. He offered no apology. When the general asked me if I was satisfied, I told him I hadn't heard an apology, and if that wasn't possible, I'd go talk to the attorneys. At that point the action officer admitted begrudgingly that perhaps he had crossed a line. Again the general asked me if I was satisfied. He was a kind and loving man, and I could see how much it pained him to be in the middle of a confrontation. I realized that was probably the best I could hope for, so I reluctantly agreed. He asked me to wait outside because he wanted to address the assignments chaplain privately. I could hear some rather heated words. As the door opened again, I heard the general say, "Go get it and bring it to me NOW!" The assignments chaplain stomped off in a snit.

The general called me back in and explained he was nominating me as the next division chaplain for the First Armored Division in Germany. However, he had not been able to get the assignments officer to send the nomination letter. That was a bit beyond my belief. I reminded him he was a two-star general and the action officer was a lieutenant colonel. "I will make the nomination personally today by telephone," he promised. I thanked him, and he informed me I would leave to take the position that summer.

In the last six months before my rotation to Germany, the assignments officer still seemed out of control. I was wrestling with the fact that he continued making remarks and spreading rumors. I began praying to acknowledge that God never made a victim, or a victimizer. Yet, I couldn't get rid of the sense of injustice. Resentment is the ultimate folly of punishing yourself for another's indiscretions.

In the new assignment I would need to do long-distance running. I had begun running the monuments on the DC Mall during lunch. Shortly after that I found I was experiencing stiffness in my hip. It seemed clear to me that the difficulty was associated with my inability to spiritually address the attacks.

Driving home one night, I implored God sincerely, meekly, to help me understand a more spiritual way ahead. I remember thinking, "I know

You are asking me to love in the face of hatred, but I know that You don't want me to approve of the public demeaning, or the dishonesty, or the revengeful acts, so I don't think You are telling me to love those sorts of things. So what is it that would impel me to love given the viciousness and frequency of his actions?" I implored Him, "How can I love him when the attacks persist?" The car seemed to become very warm, and a sense of light filled my consciousness. Then I heard these biblical words: "because he first loved us" (I John 4:19). Yes! If Jesus could say of those who were literally crucifying him, "Father, forgive them; for they know not what they do," then I knew I could forgive this, and I knew I could listen to God's Word in this matter. The hip was completely healed when I stepped out of the car at my home a few minutes later. Suddenly, it seemed clear to me that this individual had many deep waters he was going through and would go through. A short time later the man unexpectedly retired and left the army to address serious challenges in his life.

About a month later, the outgoing First Armored Division chaplain from Germany asked me to have breakfast with him at a senior leadership conference in the States. I knew him only from phone conversations. He opened our breakfast by saying he wanted me to know how the nomination had been handled on the ground in Germany. On the phone, he had agreed with the assignments chaplain in the Pentagon and subsequently wanted me to know he refused to carry my nomination to the commanding general at the First Armored Division. He had refused? My inclination at hearing this news was to be quite startled, of course.

I was still very aware of God's direction for me to be the peacemaker in this matter. I turned to God, and I heard a firm inner voice urging me, "Just listen. It isn't what you think!" I calmly and gently asked him if I had ever done anything when we worked personnel at his current or previous assignment that made him think I couldn't do the job. He responded, "Oh, heavens NO! It was nothing more than prejudice!" He explained he wanted me to know that it came to him in prayer that he was wrong. And he wanted me to know that he had then insisted on personally carrying my nomination to the division commander. It was a powerful example that prejudices can be overcome. It also came to me to ask him when this happened. It was during the very same time period as the healing of my hip. Love is powerful. In fact, I firmly believe it is the strongest power on earth.

It also seemed very odd to me that the executive officer who had protected the hateful assignments officer would ask me about five years later to write his son's letter of recommendation for active duty when he came to the Army Chaplain School for his Chaplain Officer Basic Course. My husband couldn't believe I agreed to do so. I told him that I agreed with Jeremiah's words "they shall say no more, the fathers have eaten a sour grape, and the children's teeth are set on edge" (Jeremiah 31:29). It didn't seem just that a son should be held accountable for the indiscretions of the father. We can be free of any residue from experiences that truly represent healing. There does not have to remain scars of any nature. I gladly wrote a loving and supportive letter for his son.

Good Friday—Blessed Easter in Bosnia and love wins again

It was my second tour in Germany in 1998. Our troops were in Bosnia. The Thursday before Easter, I picked up a cat we had rescued from a dumpster exactly at the same time my husband opened a can of cat food in the kitchen. He leaped from my arms. His back claws split my lip, and he opened deep wounds in my chin. At a dinner that evening our public affairs officer (PAO) ran her fingers over my chin and predicted it would leave deep scars. I immediately began to search my thought for any sense of "woundedness" that might have crept into my thought. A commander who had viciously attacked me in my previous overseas tour was back in Germany. I was prayerfully supporting an investigation into accusations of physically abusive practices in his brigade. The Ninety-First Psalm states, "I will say of the Lord, He is my refuge and my fortress: my God; in him will I trust…He shall cover thee with his feathers, and under his wings shalt thou trust: his truth shall be thy shield and buckler." It was my desire to credit God with the power to be my defense in every situation.

The next morning we flew to Bosnia to provide a Good Friday sermon for the Swedish brigade. We traveled with a rabbi who was providing Passover services for our deployed soldiers. On Saturday I studied each gospel account of the Easter events. I also looked at study passages on the biblical Easter events in Mrs. Eddy's writings. I focused my Easter sermon on how diametrically opposite the crucifixion and the resurrection events were in their intentions. For those who opposed Jesus and his teachings, the "cross" represented their collective hatred for the Christ, Truth. The "crown" or the resurrection represented Christ Jesus's all-absorbing spiritual love for mankind in his triumph over death and the grave, and that such love was indeed the way to salvation from fear or hate.

Hatred was a big issue in Bosnia, where ethnic cleansing and religious issues divided the population. Our service members were physically in danger, constantly attempting to avoid hidden minefields or improvised explosive devises (IEDs). I encouraged everyone to recognize how effective prayer could be as the armor for our hearts, quoting Mrs. Eddy's statement, "Clad in the panoply of Love, human hatred cannot reach you" (*Pulpit and Press* 15:18–19). Explaining that love's panoply was an armor that protects completely, I pointed out that this protection from hatred was not just from hatred directed at you from sources outside yourself—it was more important to understand that love protects you from hatred's getting a foothold within your own thought or heart.

I included an illustration based on the fact that redwoods grew so large and tall and lived so long, and that three characteristics made this possible. First, they had thick, resistant bark. Almost no pests or diseases could get through the bark to harm one of these trees. I compared the bark to various Christian virtues that protected the heart. Compassion, honesty, a gracious spirit, kindness, and forgiveness were just a few that protected someone from hatred entering their heart from outside sources. These large and most beautiful of trees had a second defense against harm: the root system. Each redwood in a grove sends out a comprehensive root network that intertwines with the other redwoods around it. They all support each other, and this is an exceptionally firm foundation. I likened that to our study of the scriptures and our following Jesus's admonition to love God and our neighbor. And the third reason that the redwoods often live close to a thousand years is that they never stop growing. This I used to encourage the soldiers to continue to grow in grace every day of their lives and to stay close to the scriptures.

At one point I looked out at the seats to see if the people appeared to be connecting with the message. I saw many smiles, and it seemed people were truly listening. But what surprised me most was the rabbi sitting in the front row.

Afterward, the chairman of the Joint Chiefs of Staff, our commanding general, and some of the service men and women were having breakfast in the dining facility. As we walked through to rally for our flight home, the chairman waved for me to come over to his table. I was deeply touched when he said they were still talking about the sermon. He remarked that he had heard a lot of sermons, but this was one he wouldn't forget. Then, they all recounted what illustration from the sermon they liked the best. I told them how honored I was to have been able to be with them on this special morning. I told them I felt God had fed me with the ideas I had shared.

We then made a hasty retreat to the airstrip. At that time, you only got about a seven-minute window to run out, board your plane, and take off. As we waited, the rabbi kept pointing to my chin and looking at me with a very puzzled look on his face. Verbal communication was impossible because of the noise from the air traffic. I hadn't even thought of the wounds on my face again until then. I was embarrassed that he was pointing at them. Once we were in the air, he implored me that he had to know what kind of power could heal the deep claw marks he had seen on my face. He grabbed his shaving mirror out of his duffle bag. Because there were no mirrors in Bosnia, I didn't know that the wounds had completely healed as I prepared the sermon. The sermon's ideas had made me realize I really hadn't forgiven the commander's second wave of hatred. I now had the resolve not to be pulled into this man's pattern. The rabbi shook his head, realizing I hadn't known till then that the wounds had healed.

I often think about what an impact seeing a healing has on people. Many who couldn't have contemplated such a possibility realized the greatness of God's love. It's very hard not to listen to the voice of healing when you've seen it with your own eyes.

God's leadership training at the Corps Commander's Conference

In 1999 in that same posting in Germany, one of our brigade commanders was attempting to force a young enlisted man, a chaplain assistant who was a self-proclaimed Wiccan, out of the military. That weekend our new corps commander was holding his yearly leadership conference offsite in a scenic Alpine city. At our dinner table the brigade's command sergeant major (CSM) suggested Wiccans shouldn't be allowed to serve in the army. I remarked that I thought the Constitution guaranteed Americans religious freedom. The CSM countered that in this case we should set aside the Constitution.

It was evident that other corps staff members and commanders at our table were waiting to see my response. I asked God to be the inspiration for my mouth, never wanting to be combative in such situations. God's thoughts can be both powerful and gentle. I listened, letting the silence build to the response. Then it came to me to simply ask if there were any other Constitutional amendments he and his commander intended to set aside. The redness in his face and his non-response drew a chuckle from everyone else at the table. I believe everyone, including the CSM, got the point that this was a dangerously slippery slope.

Believing that God knows everything because He is omniscient, it only seemed right to depend on Him to supply the nurturing thought needed—since He is so very good at it. I thought of the biblical assurance, "I know the thoughts that I think toward you, saith the Lord, thoughts of peace, and not of evil, to give you an expected end" (Jeremiah 29:11). That way the outcome is a blessing to all involved. Love comes to heal in such a variety of ways!

Nothing more sacred

When I was the executive director of the Armed Forces Chaplain Board (AFCB) during my second posting at the Pentagon in about 2001, I received an urgent call from the office of the chairman of the Joint Chiefs of Staff. A Bosnian contingency that was visiting the US had declined the normal briefings offered visiting international dignitaries and had asked to talk to our military chaplains. So I was asked to join the Bosnian group in the conference room. It was clear there were representatives from Muslim, Serbian, and Croatian sections of Bosnia.

Their leader's question was simple, profound, and sincere: "We all want to know how Americans of so many different religions can live and work together and not kill each other." I knew that I personally couldn't answer such a penetrating question in a satisfying manner. I also sensed that they were instinctively rejecting the idea that religious power struggles were inevitable. Something was impelling them to look for a more satisfying answer.

When I explained that in America nothing was more sacred and personal than an individual's relationship with God, they began to take notes. "We consider our military stronger and more effective when everyone is able to worship and practice their prayer disciplines in the manner they treasure," I said. "In our Albanian mission, soldiers who worked inordinate hours in the initial phase of the mission volunteered to put in additional hours to assemble our chapel."

I also recounted that in our Kosovo mission in 1999, I had helped our general understand why the United Arab Emirates (UAE) personnel couldn't worship where other non-Abraham traditions worshipped. He immediately approved a separate chapel structure for the Muslims in our operations. That responsiveness to their religious needs made an impression on all the Muslims in the Allied Forces involved in our peacemaking missions. Our visitors began to grasp that the desire to understand each other's love for God had united us. In effect, we had vigorously resisted the belief that many different human minds had to be at odds. They were encouraged and said they would work together to find solutions for persons of faith that would bless everyone.

I added that we viewed moral courage as superior to mere physical courage. The military professional ethic included the belief that a respect for the human rights protected by Geneva Convention agreements also empowered rather than restricted our military. And in closing, I underlined that the mission statements for those task forces had been "Peacemaking Missions."

It was evident that we all left the meeting that day more convinced than ever of the validity of the New Testament's assurance, "Blessed are the peacemakers: for they shall be called the children of God." When love triumphs over hate, everyone is the victor.

And now, at the Pentagon, I and all of us there were going to have to put this practice of love to the test.

September 11, 2001: A defining event of love for the home of the brave

When I recall the events of September 11, 2001, and the immediate days following, the most striking and vivid difference that stands out to me would be the comparison between what the architects of those events intended the events to be, and what, indeed, was their result. The presence of love, from God and reflected in a multitude of human ways, guided so much of what happened when hatred attempted to dominate our nation.

Extremists intended to kill countless people and strike a decisive blow to America's resolve to globalize its economic and political relationships. Terrorism by definition would intend to plant fear and would claim that hatred is a force of grave and powerful impact. They wanted the day to be remembered for defining their hatred for us and our way of life.

What indeed happened in America in those pivotal days was just the opposite. What we saw was the truly amazing response of the American people. Countless acts of heroic courage would transform dire circumstances in New York, Pennsylvania, and Washington, DC, into defining events of love for those affected by the events.

I had delved deeply into the beliefs that dominate Abrahamic groups' decisions and motivations in historical events that had caused problems for nearly fifteen years. The military had begun to listen to various voices like mine, but none of us knew the extent of a threat that was going to be imminent. Still, it was some satisfaction to me to have "said a word in season." Here is that event and its background.

When God opens the door—You Brief: Always new territory

In this second Pentagon assignment, in January and February of 2001, I worked for a navy admiral who also saw my presentation on divine command morality, the extremist mindset. She urged me to find a way to get the widest possible dissemination of the briefing. She lamented that she didn't know who would listen to a woman personnel officer and a woman chaplain in the Pentagon. She specifically suggested that I should see if I could get it seen by the joint staff.

One afternoon I headed off to the area of the Pentagon where the operations officers for the chairman of the Joint Chiefs of Staff worked. I asked some operations officers where the threat assessment section might be. They gave me an office designation, but I couldn't find the area. It wasn't marked the way other areas in the Pentagon were. I paused and listened, and then I thought of the passage from Revelation 3:8, "behold, I have set before thee an open door, and no man can shut it." At that moment, a janitor came out of an unmarked door, propping the door open with a waste receptacle. I realized it was exactly the office I needed to find. I walked in and asked who had the responsibility for the region that included Iraq. A major pointed to a couple of guys in a cubicle further back in that section. I walked up to the two officers and told them that the admiral I worked for wanted me to acquaint them with a briefing I had on Iraq. I launched into my brief, and it wasn't long before a couple of other nearby officers rolled their chairs closer so they could also hear. Afterward, they took me to places I never knew existed in the Pentagon.

In February of 2001, my admiral took me to Tampa to the Central Command (CENTCOM) headquarters. I briefed in a Video Tele-Conference (VTC) for commanders deployed in Saudi Arabia, Kuwait, and some other related task forces. Joint staff officers from the Pentagon also accompanied us.

Once again, I was aggressively attacked by one of the navy commanders in the VTC deployed in the Middle East region. He accused me of being prejudiced and vehemently explained that the Muslims in his area would never hurt anyone. He wanted to extend the tours, making them family-accompanied tours. I reassured him the briefing only applied to a small percentage of extremists in Abraham traditions. I reiterated that included Christian and Jewish manifestations of the mindset that have historically caused their governments problems.

At this point, the general running the briefings intervened. He worked directly for the CENTCOM commanding general. He asked the joint staff and his officers to give their opinions of the value of the briefing. I was relieved when the officers in the room lauded the briefing. I was asked to provide slides and a manuscript. They wanted General Tommy Franks, who was constantly in the news in that period, to read the brief. The Joint Chiefs of Staff team who accompanied us also asked if I would help them by doing a similar analysis of Osama Bin Laden.

I told them I would if my admiral agreed. I explained this type of analysis wasn't my day job, and I didn't have access to the classified documents they had on Osama Bin Laden. They mentioned that one of the things that had really struck them about the briefing was my sources were all "open sources." They mentioned that they were very impressed by the insights and examples I had included from the *Christian Science Monitor*. They were familiar with the newspaper, but now they saw its value for them in understanding people's mindsets that were very different from those the armed forces usually dealt with.

When we returned to the Pentagon, my admiral told me the deputy secretary of defense was very pleased with the results of the trip. He had opposed the commanders who wanted to bring our families into the region, but had not been able to articulate his reservations about it. He asked for my slides and subsequently didn't approve the extensions of the tours to include families. Although we had no way of knowing it, we could have spent huge amounts of money to move the families overseas that summer; then, by September, terrorists would have attacked America. And at that time, post-September 11, 2001, it would have no doubt required an immediate extraction of our family members from those regions at an extraordinary cost.

But now I continued to pray to support an intelligent analysis of threats looming on the horizon from those following the divine command mindset. Then the moment arrived when the threats would present themselves as startling reality.

For me the memories start vividly the evening before. Leaving the Metro that evening, my thought was drawn to the repetitive rolling thunder of a huge gathering storm. It was one of those rare times I felt God was directing my thought. Initially I assumed he was teaching me that I shouldn't pray that such destructive elements would go around me but hit somewhere else. Then, the voice became even more distinctive and urgent, prompting me to "pray about the gathering of malice."

Immediately a passage from *Science and Health* by Mary Baker Eddy, burned brightly in my thought: "There is too much animal courage in society and not sufficient moral courage" (28:31–1). Then another related idea of Mrs. Eddy's in that same book came to thought. She makes a further distinction that "God governs all that is real, harmonious, and eternal, and His power is neither animal nor human" (102:2–3). That led my thought to pray to acknowledge the fact that moral courage is superior to animal courage. The urging to pray remained very insistent all that evening. I prayed until nearly one o'clock that morning. Every day I am more and more sure that such prayers of acknowledgment bring the truth of God's power to bear in very tangible ways.

That next morning I got a call from the Pentagon dental clinic for my annual examination. The receptionist apologized that she hadn't called me on 8-11, my birthday. She remarked that somehow my file had gotten lost on her desk for exactly one month. That call pulled me to the opposite side of the Pentagon. As I left my office, the voice I heard in prayer again directed me to go back and get my weekly Bible lesson. I did that and went to the appointment.

The clinics had CNN monitors. As I waited for the results of my panoramic X-rays, we all saw the early footage of the plane flying into the first tower of the World Trade Center. Like the majority of Americans, we debated what could have gone wrong. Then a chilling silence fell over the room when the other plane hit the second tower. Everyone had pretty much realized this had to be a terrorist attack.

Someone ran in and said we had to evacuate the Pentagon because a plane had also hit our building. For a moment we thought people might have been confused by what they were seeing happening in New York. But the person said, "No, a plane has hit our building," and ordered us to evacuate.

I found two other chaplains near the entrance of the Pentagon athletic club. One of the men had tried to go back into the Pentagon, but the security guards had threatened to arrest him. We held hands and prayed. I shared that in my prayer I was assured our right place was to be with the casualties. I insisted that the book of Revelation stated, "I have set before thee an open door, and no man can shut it" (Revelation 3:8). We all agreed we had to be there for the casualties.

The medical teams were forming behind us. As the senior chaplain, I suggested we'd fall in with the medical teams. When one of the doctors yelled, "Medical Team number one, GO! Medical Team number two, GO!" we each fell in with one of the teams.

When we reached the security turnstiles, the guards attempted to stop us. I knew the head of security because I often made homemade cookies for the guards who worked holidays. So I stepped forward and said, "Mike, this is doctrinal that chaplains go with the medical teams to pray with the casualties." He immediately recognized me, and he smiled and said, "Okay, Chaplain Horton, you guys can go in." Then we were allowed to run on into "Ground Zero," the center courtyard of the Pentagon where the firemen were just beginning to bring out our casualties.

In the military you never simply assume someone wants to pray. Out of respect for their mental privacy, you ask if they would like to. When we talked later, it had struck each of us that not one person said no. Next, we would ask the person's faith background and would kneel on the grass beside them and pray in terms familiar and meaningful from their tradition. Often the words of the Twenty-Third Psalm seemed all too pertinent, "He maketh me to lie down in green pastures…He restoreth my soul…Yea, though I walk through the valley of the shadow of death, I will fear no evil: for thou art with me." This was almost eerie because the firemen were bringing people out and placing them on the green grass in that inner courtyard. The plane had hit the building and crashed through the outer three rings. The fire was burning hotly out front. Therefore, from the inner courtyard the firemen were able to approach the areas where there were more survivors in the inner two rings of that wedge.

I found the Christian Science weekly Bible lesson (Section V) for September 11 focused on reducing fear and inflammation. Those ideas were particularly relevant for the needs of the casualties. I started paraphrasing and putting the verses into the first person as if they were being spoken directly to each casualty. From Malachi 3:6 and 4:2 I shared "I am the Lord, I change not; therefore [you shall not be] consumed. But… the Sun of righteousness [shall] arise with healing in his wings." And from Jeremiah 30:10, 17: "Fear not…neither be dismayed,… for…I will save [you] from afar, and…[you] shall return, and [you] shall be in rest, and be quiet, and none shall make [you] afraid…For I will restore health unto [you], and I will heal [you] of [your] wounds, saith the Lord." I also prayed to know that God understands all things and to Him all things are possible. One of the correlative study passages in the Christian Science textbook read, "To reduce inflammation…I have found divine Truth more potent than all lower remedies" (*Science and Health* 180:31–1)

One of the earliest casualties I prayed with had taken a break from a meeting and gone to the men's room down the corridor. When the fuel in the plane exploded, he found he was on fire. He spoke of that moment in a Pentagon prayer breakfast months later. As the terror of what was happening hit him, he said his first thought was that he would never see his family again. He fought this horrible suggestion with a wise and discerning heart. He recognized it as the temptation to die. That impelled his heart to turn to God in prayer. He affirmed that he loved his wife and kids and wanted to live to see them again. As his heart yielded to God's possibility in the scenario, he felt the sprinklers activate. The rush of water put out flames that had engulfed him. He was then able to crawl out of the restroom doors toward the closed fire doors in the innermost ring. Two other officers I prayed with from the A ring had run from the engulfing smoke and expanding flames. Yet they were concerned and called to see if anyone was down that corridor and being stopped by the fire door. They managed to break open the door and get a person part of the way out before they were overcome by smoke. To everyone's blessing, the smoke-masked firemen quickly carried them out into the Pentagon courtyard.

They were some of the earliest casualties retrieved. One of the colonels was kneeling and taking in oxygen as I arrived. He selflessly insisted I should go on to others who were far more seriously hurt than he. I knelt beside the officer who had been on fire, and he said he wanted to pray.

The Bible passages seemed to comfort him. I continued on to other casualties being put on the grass.

Nearly every casualty seemed to calm noticeably as soon as they heard the familiar and comforting words of the scriptures. One woman who was Catholic wanted to repeat the "Our Father." It was a sweet and moving moment I will never forget.

One man I knelt beside told me he was Baptist. I smiled and said I was sure he would want to pray. He agreed vigorously, but he seemed transfixed by the attempts of the medical team removing his socks and cutting his pants away from his legs. He kept repeating, loudly and emotionally, that he could see what they were doing, but he couldn't feel his legs. He had jumped from a second-story window to escape the fire from the exploding airplane fuel. I was told later that as he lay on the cement below, unable to move from the waist down, he had used his arms to break the fall of others jumping from the second-story window in his office.

It concerned me that the lieutenant colonel, unlike any other casualty, wasn't calming down. I turned to God and listened for what I could do. It came to me to speak to him with more authority. So I paraphrased Romans 8:38, 39: "Now Marion, you listen to me! [Nothing] can separate you from the love of God, which is in Christ Jesus, …[neither]…height, nor depth, nor things present, nor things to come, nor principalities, nor powers." When he heard those familiar, comforting, and beloved words of the Scripture, he calmed down decidedly.

Just then we were told there might be another unaccounted-for airplane. We were instructed to move everyone out to the Potomac, where ambulances were arriving to evacuate the casualties. As we lifted the officer onto the litter, some dried leaves were poking one of his legs. He began to exclaim loudly, "OUCH!" There was a moment when we all realized that this indicated he was feeling his legs, and we simultaneously threw our hands in the air and rejoiced. I was relieved when I called him a few weeks later. He told me he had some issues with his ankles, and yet he had already returned to work.

A young specialist had put out the fire on a civilian woman and pulled her up through the crumbling floor. He carried her to the window and saved her from the rapidly expanding fireball mushrooming through their office area. He got her out of the window onto the walkway below. She was also one of the early casualties I prayed with at Ground Zero. I wouldn't see her again until I retired in Ocala, Florida. She recalled our prayer and just wanted to talk to someone who had been there that day. I joined her at a benefit at the Ocala Hilton, where she encouraged others who had sustained brain damage that they could win their way back.

Early on, I encountered a navy operations center NCO desperately searching for survivors of her unit. She was on a mail run when the plane hit. She had realized the plane had landed directly on her section, and yet she was determined to see if anyone had seen any navy survivors. You could hear the emotion and grief as she ran from person to person. I held her by her shoulders and told her the people we were assisting were alive and they needed our help. I assured her there would also be an appropriate time for everyone to grieve later. Her military training immediately kicked in, and she wholeheartedly dove into assisting with the casualties.

People often ask me if I was afraid as we worked. I have always said that fear was a selfish emotion. I don't recall anyone that day among the responders who appeared to be afraid. It seemed clear to me they were so focused on helping others that they weren't thinking about themselves. They were totally immersed in what the next casualty would need, or what they could do to protect the children in the childcare facility, or if they could identify who was unaccounted for. Instead of fear, what we did see was an absolute unity of effort, love in action.

Because no one working the site had anything to eat or drink, the military police shot the locks off the soda machines to get something for the firemen to drink. Chaplains and other workers poured out the soda and filled the bottles with water. When a bin of ice we were pushing across the cement tipped over, I was struck by seeing a two-star air force general, a young specialist, and myself, a colonel, working side by side to instantly scoop up the ice and get the job done. Not one person groused about the job being inappropriate to their rank or that someone else should be doing a menial job. It was an inspired effort by everyone.

Some of us broke into the snack bar and scrounged for food. We found a few hamburger buns. A surprising picture resulted. The chaplains began to serve the firemen. It was the first time I saw any of them taking even a moment to sit down. We went from fireman to fireman, breaking bread, the hamburger rolls, and handing them a cup of cold water. Many of them remarked that it felt like a holy communion.

Later, when we had evacuated all the casualties, a priest from Fort

Myer and I went out to check on the children in the childcare facility. A very inspired effort from the marines and the workers resulted in the hasty movement of the children into the trees in the park near the Potomac River. We found that most of the children had been successfully reunited with their parents. We returned to the center courtyard and awaited the change from casualty assistance to mortuary affairs.

At that one small break late in the afternoon, an air force officer gave a special Pentagon cell phone to those of us working the site, for us to pass around. We would finally have an opportunity to inform our families that we were okay. I don't recall anyone's number ringing more than once. The families were glued to the phones waiting for any kind of information or call. We each assured our loved ones we were not hurt, and then quickly passed the phone to the next person waiting.

On an average day about twenty-four thousand people work in the Pentagon, and a couple thousand visitors arrive throughout the day. Yet it was amazing how limited the casualties were that day. It was a common story for someone to say, I had just gone for the mail or coffee or a meeting. The plane hit a Pentagon wedge that was being renovated. Twice in the previous months we thought we were going to move into our new offices. Once we didn't go because the computers weren't ready, and another time there was a delay with the furniture. As it was, the diagrams that showed where the plane exploded put the nose of the plane just behind the Pentagon library. If you walked out the front of the library, you were at the front door of our temporary office!

I found out later that my secretary had felt the impact and jumped up from her desk. She stepped into the hall to see a huge cloud of smoke and debris flying through the air toward her. She ran out the opposite direction. She left when security told people to leave the area and go home. When we finally returned to our office space, there was a lot of debris and pieces of the ceiling on the desk and floor of my inner office area. It took several days before my secretary could bring herself to return to the building. It was such a common response that we found it helpful to station a chaplain at the Metro entrance. It was not unusual to find the need to minister to those facing the fears of returning to work in the building.

The Armed Forces Chaplains Board (AFCB) was a joint office, supervised by the office of the Undersecretary for Personnel and Readiness. The personnel office crunched the numbers on the casualties. I have a copy of the original run on the numbers. The office estimated that 196 people were missing. That included the unconfirmed count of 64 persons on the American Airlines flight 77. Compared to the numbers in the thousands we were hearing from New York, that seemed miraculous to everyone.

Most people theorized that the plane didn't hit the section of the Pentagon that it was targeting. It appeared the inexperienced pilot had spun in a bit too early. He came down over the Navy Annex and hit the wedge near the helipad that faced Crystal City. The opposite side of the Pentagon is considered the high-rent district. It would have been the most probable place to target in the building. That section contained the offices for the service secretaries as well as the chairman of the Joint Chiefs of Staff. Their eighth and ninth corridor offices went untouched.

When I talked to my chaplain friends later, none of us remembered exactly how we got out of Ground Zero. We all remembered wading through water that was building up in the inner ring sidewalks as the fire crews continued to drench the building. The Metro at the Pentagon was closed, and thousands of people had to find other means of getting home. The day's impact had already begun to show in the generosity of the DC area drivers. Taxis and individuals in personal vehicles compassionately started offering free rides to people stranded in the Pentagon area.

The chaplain coverage in the next few weeks would indeed be a joint and total effort by all the services. We all worked together, tirelessly providing some of the most diverse forms of ministry we'd seen in our careers. Almost immediately a village sprang up in the parking lot that faced the Pentagon City Mall. The FBI and other intelligence agencies also began to work the site. To feed the hundreds who worked almost continuously for the next few weeks, McDonalds, Outback Steakhouse, and a church's rotisserie chicken group provided food free of charge to anyone in the recovery teams. We also set up a tent where fire and rescue workers could see their families on the few breaks that they took.

Later, when a mortuary affairs officer was briefing the volunteers from The Old Guard from Fort Myer, we witnessed an incredible turning of thought. The Old Guard is an elite unit of military members, handpicked for the burial teams at Arlington Cemetery. To be selected for this duty at Arlington Cemetery, they had to be visually what was considered "picture perfect" soldiers. They were standing tall until the officer began to describe what their duties would be. He explained that you had to volunteer for this difficult duty and that there wouldn't be any stigma if anyone found it a duty too difficult to stomach. However, as he began to describe what the duties would entail, he began to get so graphic it appeared to be affecting the majority of the troops. You could see some getting woozy or nauseous. Some soldiers had already begun to take a step backward, indicating they were reconsidering volunteering.

At this point a somewhat shy Catholic priest stepped forward. (This was completely out of character compared to his normal unassuming manner.) He interrupted the briefer and exclaimed with deep emotion and compassion in his voice, "That's not what you're going in there to do. You're going in there (he pointed to the Pentagon wedge damaged by the crash and fire) to bring the precious remains of our families' loved ones out of the darkness into the light. Then we will be able to honor them in the manner appropriate for the ultimate sacrifice they made for their country." Needless to say, every one of the Old Guard soldiers stepped forward proudly and stated they would volunteer.

The recovery teams insisted they would not go without a chaplain. Whenever they found anything even remotely resembling human remains, they knelt, and the chaplain with the team provided a blessing.

The chaplains worked together to establish a joint family assistance center at a nearby Sheraton Hotel to support the families who lost dear ones in the Pentagon. The families were anxiously waiting to have it confirmed that their loved ones' remains were recoverable. We also helped them arrange for military burials and appropriate funerals for the civilian workers lost.

The military were all at work the next morning. The leadership wanted to send a message, as a show of resolve, that the Pentagon was fully functioning. Some people had been so impressed by the repetitive images of the planes flying into the World Trade Centers that they were having trouble sleeping. Large numbers of adult counselees had watched the plane fly into the Pentagon from the sidewalks or as they drove into the parking lots. They also had problems shaking the images of the explosion. A number of moms and dads said their children were having nightmares and asked what they could do. I suggested replacing the repetitively disturbing pictures with a favorite song. Everyone can identify with how a favorite song tends to stick in your head once you've sung it. We tried "Jesus loves me this I know, for the Bible tells me so" or a favorite hymn. I was told by a number of families that it not only worked wonderfully for the children but also was helpful to them.

A few days later, President Bush was scheduled to speak to the nation about America's response to these shocking events. The White House wanted someone who had been at the Pentagon to sit with Mrs. Bush. I was asked to email a copy of the Bible lesson passages to a presidential liaison. By Thursday morning I was told I was one of two people being considered to sit with Laura Bush. I was told to be ready in my class "A" uniform. About five o'clock I was informed I had been chosen. I'm not really quite sure why, but I asked who the other person was being considered. The liaison said it was a young enlisted man. I knew of the heroic nature of the young man's actions that day, and I felt moved to ask if it was too late to let him have the opportunity. I was asked why, in a shocked voice. I said that I was at the very end of my career. This dear enlisted man was at the beginning of his. This opportunity would grace him immeasurably throughout his career. I was moved to tears when they agreed to let him go to sit with Mrs. Bush.

The Pentagon chief historian had the monumental task of recording the amazing things people had done in the building that day. He asked me to allow him to keep the original Bible lesson booklet I shared with the casualties that day. He was very taken by the applicability and timeliness of the passages. He was amazed by the fact they were prepared months in advance. I found it hard to give up something that meant so much to me, but I realized it needed to go into the historical record of the day. He told me he couldn't remember seeing anyone more emotionally moved when having to part with an item for the archives.

In June 2002, I was asked to be part of a ceremony to honor the fire and rescue workers who had responded to our needs in the Pentagon on September 11, 2001. I was told that the firemen had remembered the lady chaplain and asked if I would provide their invocation. I was also delighted to find that the Old Dominion District Boy Scouts from the National Capitol Region would be present to honor the men who were a part of an elite battalion of rescue workers. This is the same elite battalion that responded for the Hurricane Andrew rescue efforts in Florida and the earthquakes in Mexico in recent years.

I spent a number of days praying about what to put into that important invocation. As I sat in my home one evening, a poem began to rush into my consciousness. It was all I could do to record the words pouring into my thought. I knew God, divine Love, was leading me in this important tasking. I printed the poem on parchment and placed a commemorative stamp depicting the firemen raising the American flag on September 11. The stamp read, "Heroes USA." This is the poem I offered at the dinner on June 14, 2002.

"The Best in Human Character"
The Fairfax County Search and Rescue Team

Almighty and Merciful God,
How great a task it is to offer prayer
For humble servants who come to bear
In many times through constant care
Faithfully, they're always there
In each day upon them cast your ever-watchful eye.

For in their neighbor's time of need
Not one just simply passes by.
They find and rescue in distress so dire
Oft' in times of earthquake, wind and fire.
And unknown dangers cannot stay
Because You preserve them in the way.

In this a free and open land
Where freedom flows from hand to hand
There duty done lifts hearts on high
As stars and stripes so boldly fly
An emblem of their selflessness,
A spirit pure, and blessedness
Their kind and tender manner
Would constitute their banner.
Theirs is a courageous work
Never deterred when dangers lurk.
The best in human character they show
And most of us would hardly know.
Their valor's rarely e'er perceived
In recognition well deserved.

To our ideals and values hold.
This is the American spirit, bold
To rise, to help and heal.
We this evening now reveal
To look on them with gratitude
For brave and noble fortitude.
For duty done and valor lived
We thank them Lord and ask You give
Your recognition e'en divine.
The fire only can refine
Their hearts and souls to serve Thee more
Your greater purpose now.
For rescue workers, living and deceased
We ask your blessings, grace and peace.

When my church asked me to record how that day changed or affected me, I wrote these observations:

The weapons that counter terror are spiritual, and are "mighty through God to the pulling down of strongholds; Casting down imaginations" (II Corinthians 10:4–5). The truest form of enemy that must be countered is not personal. It is anything that would claim hatred, animosity, or violence can ever be God's power or will. It is hatred we must learn to defeat. Love is the most powerful weapon and shield that can be used to defeat malice in any form. It was love for one's neighbor, selflessness, moral courage, and generosity that defeated the intentions of terrorists on September 11. It was the incarnation of the Word, that none simply passed by in their neighbor's time of need.

Such love, a reflection of God's absolute love for his creation, can't be stopped. It truly is power. It undergirds our effort to comfort the brokenhearted, to restore sight to those who are blind to the good in others. It can destroy sin and fear. It is amazing in its graciousness and its ability to neutralize anything unlike it. It is the only sovereign power and is the clear manifestation of God's law of love. We must want to be a force leading all nations and all peoples to a present and clearer recognition and knowledge of their spiritual identity. This unity is profound and attainable. We must be a voice rousing mankind to join in the recognition that it is attainable.

I will never be in the same place I was before those events. I am more alert and more clearly at a position of attention, spiritually. I am wiser in my prayer: It is quieter; it is deeper in its protests for truth against any erroneous concept of man that limits our sense of brotherhood. I am listening more obediently in prayer and doing less outlining for God. I am surer today than ever before that He is a very present help in trouble. And I am listening and knowing He is willing and able to lead us each step of the way through His defining love.

These were experiences that refined the love I needed to have for my fellow chaplains, service members, and civilians. Christ Jesus also noted it was easy to love those who love you. Loving in the face of hatred is far more demanding but worth every effort it takes to do so. I grew spiritually because I walked those tough roads and climbed some pretty steep hills. What I learned was that we don't walk or climb alone, and that the truly high roads and steep climbs must be scaled with God's guiding and sustaining hand to enable us to be a tangible example of love overcoming hate.

Still, there were military assessments to be made. I was a colonel in the United States army and we needed to brief and to prepare to forestall another such catastrophe.

The Value Becomes Apparent

I had no idea how often I would be asked to provide the ever-expanding presentation on DCM, the mindset behind 9/11. None of us knew that future world events would draw even more attention to the distinctions it explained.

Within the week I was asked to brief "Checkmate," the name given the planners in the Air Force Operations Center (AFOC) who were putting together military plans to respond to the attacks in New York and the Pentagon and the plane brought down in Pennsylvania.

Shortly after that I was also asked to brief the Army Operations Center (AOC). The chaplain planner escorted me to the briefing area. When I finished the briefing, I was very honored that the officers and civilians in the AOC gave me a big round of applause. I wasn't expecting that, so I asked the chaplain planner if that was customary. He told me it was the first time he had ever known it to happen, and I was downright shocked. It was a very encouraging moment I'll never forget.

Because the word about the briefing got around, I pretty much made the rounds of the federal agencies in DC. I provided training for the Joint Military Intelligence College, the Threat and Assessment team for CIA, a member of the National Security Council, the Office of the Secretary of Defense General Counsel members preparing to set up the commission to try GITMO detainees, the Department of Justice, and the National Ground Intelligence Center (now the National Intelligence University). After I retired I was invited to speak at the US Marshals Office and later at Pace University in New York City for students and professors who teach the homeland defense curriculum.

The most common response I've received was that my presentation wasn't like any other briefing they'd seen. Many said that things they hadn't understood before were now more understandable. If I was any part of helping people understand each other's beliefs, then I believe it was worth the study, effort, and travel.

The experiences of 9/11 and the months thereafter would forever mark me and greatly deepen my faith. Three years later I would retire from active duty, taking all of the experiences I had had in America's armed forces with me. However, the day when love triumphed over the hatred and destructive planning of terrorists will always top my list of memorable times.

One cherished sisterhood

As the time for retirement neared, I recalled the time in 1993 when, as I was promoted to lieutenant colonel (LTC), I was privileged to have Chaplain (Major General) Matthew Zimmerman conduct my promotion ceremony. To my delight Diana, my roommate in basic training and dear friend, was able to join me. I had so treasured being at her promotion a few months earlier. Chaplain Zimmerman conducted the ceremony like a proud father, and my husband Jeff and Diana pinned on my silver oak leaves. I began to think at that time that the predictions back in Chaplain Officer Basic Course that neither she nor I would make it because of the double whammy of minority factors had now been laid to rest. I looked forward to our continuing to prove the skeptics wrong. It was especially meaningful that Diana was with me at that ceremony at the Women's Memorial.

Leaving the service was a time to assess the road behind us, and the road ahead, particularly for women. As my career had progressed, despite the predictions it wouldn't happen, there were many levels of recogni-

-tion. When a woman chaplain's performance was impressive, the true professionals and chaplains with sincerely loving hearts acknowledged your accomplishments. Some of them may have even borne criticism for doing so, but they chose to take the high road and provide coaching and mentoring for us.

However, some individuals were more extreme in their resistance. When egos or envy were mixed into the equation, there was a more personal feel to the resistance. Throughout an entire career you needed to be vigilant to identify hatred when it became a factor. At those moments, prayer was the most effective defense. I think that most of the women chaplains realized that what one learned in the crucible was yet another step in the progress we sought to be a part of.

So much had been accomplished. After twenty-eight years of service in the army, it was apparent that the new idea of women being military chaplains had indeed been born and acknowledged as just and practicable through the inspired work of a core group of workers in the vineyard. With this fulfillment in mind, I could leave the service with a sense of satisfaction and gratitude.

Just before his crucifixion and resurrection, Jesus Christ gave his followers this counsel in the gospel of John (12:26): "Whoever serves me must follow me, and where I am, my servant also will be. My Father will honor the one who serves me." It was my honor to serve our Lord and to do so in the US Army.

AFTERWORD

In the years after I left the service, the idea of women as successful military chaplains would mature into full bloom without promotional ceilings for both the air force and navy chaplains. Women served as chiefs of chaplains in both these branches by 2013. But a woman has never been selected to serve in the highest position in the army chaplaincy. Because at this writing the new army deputy chief of chaplains for the army is once again a man, the opportunity for a woman army chief of chaplains won't open again until at least 2024. Even then, it may or may not occur. Yet on that day, when the highest office in the chaplaincy of the United States Army is offered to a woman, all women who previously served in the army chaplaincy will join their voices in praise for the day we all worked to be a part of. For all of us, we can find comfort in knowing we were in small ways a part of that collective accomplished that advanced women's rights in our beloved country. It is satisfying to realize that we all joined together to make history—to establish equity and opportunity for all in our army chaplaincy.

Glossary of Military Terms

AET (Asymmetrical Ethical Threats). Threat forces with ethics that drive their actions that are qualitatively different from dominant Western-European cognitive or non-cognitive ethics which prevalently form the basis of American mindsets.

AFCB (Armed Forces Chaplain Board). A Department of Defense Board composed of the three major generals who are the army, air force, and navy/marine chief of chaplains who govern regulatory publications and work issues that are common to all military chaplains.

AFOC or AOC (Air Force or Army Operations Center). Briefing centers for the secretary of the air force or the secretary of the army in the pentagon. A body of high-ranking officers with combat experience who prepare for and construct any military responses by the air force or the army.

ASG (Area Support Group). The military units that support service members, authorized civilians, and family members deployed overseas with any non-combat functions as well as military housing, shopping marts, etc. with English-speaking workers.

ATC (Artillery Training Center). The army's artillery school at Fort Sill, Oklahoma, where officers and enlisted train for artillery occupational specialties.

AWOL (Absent Without Leave). Not at your appointed place of duty without being on official leave or away for temporary duty from your assigned military unit.

BOQ (Bachelor Officer Quarters). Military apartments for single officers.

CAD (Combined Arms Department). Combat arms officers (infantry, artillery, armor, or air defense artillery) who teach combat support or combat service support officers their basic military skills in other branch specialty officer training courses. The instructors provide training such as map reading, weapons qualification, leadership, and field survival training.

CETCOM (US Army Central Command). One of the major command headquarters commanded by a four-star general, which was located in Tampa, Florida, at the time of the briefing.

Chairman of the Joint Chiefs of Staff. The senior general who holds the office of chairman, who is one of the chiefs of staff of one of the military service branches. The position is rotated among the army, navy, and air force. The general commands the US military forces at the Department of Defense level in the Pentagon.

Chaplain. A non-combatant professional branch officer who performs or provides for the religious support of service members, their families, and authorized civilians on military installations in the continental United States or in areas overseas where the military is deployed or in combat operations. Churches/religious faith traditions ordain or endorse their religious ministry professionals and lend them to the US military to perform or coordinate for the religious needs of those in military operations.

Chaplain Assistant. A combatant enlisted soldier who assists the military chaplain on the battlefield or in the garrison settings. The soldier is a trained combatant who qualifies with a weapon to provide for the security of the chaplain in military operations. He also provides clerical support in the chapel setting, maintains the ministry team's vehicle, supervises the set up for varied religious services, and provides any other support the chaplain needs to maintain religious support for all soldiers.

Classified Documents. Military intelligence documents are classified to identify what level of security clearance is needed for a person to have access to the information in the document. Secret, Top Secret, and higher levels of clearances are needed to read or handle such documents under any circumstances. These type of documents are guarded by military police when not in appropriately secure facilities or safes.

CG (Commanding General). The highest operational general who is in charge of a division, corps, or high-level task force for the army.

Corps. One of the highest army operational headquarters commanded by a lieutenant general, consisting of two or more divisions and auxiliary arms and services.

CGSC (Command and General Staff College). A mid-level military school that prepares select majors or new lieutenant colonels to be staff officers for general officers who command large military organizations such as divisions, corps, or other large task force organizations.

DCSPER (Deputy Chief of Staff for Personnel). The lieutenant general who supervises all personnel matters for the army.

DISCOM (Division Support Command). A large support brigade that provides maintenance, communications, transportation, etc., to combat brigades.

1st SGT (First Sergeant). The senior or "Top" sergeant who supervises a company-size unit (about two hundred service members). The nickname for the 1st SGT is often "Top."

IED (Improvised Explosive Device). Handmade bombs made by improvising with any available explosives and shrapnel, etc.

In-processing. The paperwork necessary for a personnel transfer from one military unit to any other military unit to ensure pay and compensations and accountability are maintained for the service member and family

Installation Chaplain. The highest-ranking chaplain on any large army base or facility who supervises all lower-ranking chaplains and enlisted chaplain assistants and the delivery of religious support to the military and families in that area.

JAG (Judge Advocate General). The legal corps of attorneys and judges in the military.

Joint Staff. A body within the Department of Defense that consists of senior service members from all the branches (army, navy/marines, air force, and coast guard) that advise the secretary of defense on military operations and issues.

M-16 rifle. A standard issue military rifle in the 1970s through about 2005.

MP (Military Police)

MTA (Massachusetts Transit Authority). The subway system in Boston, Massachusetts.

Metro. The name for the subway system in Washington, DC.

Medevac. Medical evacuation vehicle, a helicopter or ground transportation for service members needing medical services.

NCO (Non-Commissioned Officer). Any enlisted army service member who is appointed to a non-commissioned grade, from corporal to the sergeant major of the army.

NCOIC (Non-Commissioned Officer in Charge). The enlisted sergeant of senior rank who is the supervisor in a work section.

OER (Officer Evaluation Report). Normally a yearly performance evaluation of an officer by his immediate supervisory leader, the rater, and that leader's supervisor/the senior rater. An intermediate chaplain rating is also provided by a chaplain who would supervise religious support from the next higher military level of that organization. In chaplain organizations, two chaplains may be the rater and senior rater.

OML (Order of Merit List). The list of selectees on a military selection board that shows who received the highest to lowest ratings from the board members.

PAO (Public Affairs Officer). The officer that coordinates or conducts media contacts with military units, installations, etc.

PT (Physical Training). Runs, workouts, or any physical exercise that is often done in formation with coworkers or the entire military unit of assignment.

RIA (Religious Impact Analysis). An analysis of the impact that the use of religious symbols or ideas has in a particular area of operations.

SPO (Support Operations Officer). The officer who plans and supervises all the military operations or training exercises for the division's support command.

UMT (Unit Ministry Team). The chaplains and chaplain assistants that provide religious support at all levels of the military.

VTC (Video Tele-Conference). The video and audio telecast to multiple stations of a group meeting, which allows discussion and a visual to all participating stations.

VFW (Veterans of Foreign Wars). Local clubs established by veterans who fought and served in the US military in overseas military campaigns, wars, and conflicts.

WAC (Women's Army Corps). The auxiliary corps where women served as administrative workers and other specialties other than medical/nursing fields until 1974.

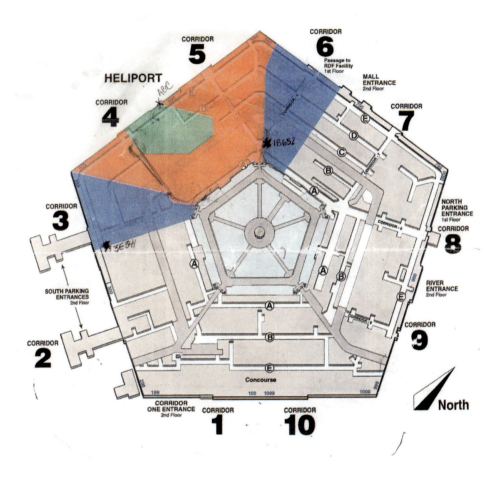

The five-sided Pentagon Building has nested rings, A, B, C, D, & E. The green area indicates structural damage, the orange area indicates the fire damage area and the blue areas indicate the water and smoke damage sections. Corridors divide each of the sections in two. The plane, American Airlines Flight 77, struck the E, D, and C rings of the 4th and 5th corridor areas. My office was on the first floor of the B ring in the 6th corridor indicated by the *IB652.

This illustration of the Pentagon on 9/11 shows a diagram of the place at which the plane entered the building complex and the spot the nose of the plane ended up as it exploded.

A close-up shot of the 4th Corridor damage shows that the concrete and steel structure had been blown apart by the volumn of fuel that exploded in the plane when it crashed into the Pentagon structure. My dear friend General Timothy Maude's office was in this section. It was here that he "gave his all" for his country.

My dear "sister in arms" Chaplain (LtC Ret.) Diana McNiel James once again joined me at the Women's Memorial at my retirement ceremony.

Brigadier General Wilma L. Vaught (Ret) posed with my husband Jeff and me after speaking about our ground-breaking work to make women's uniforms more functional. She was herself a ground-breaking founder of the Women In Military Service for America Memorial where my retirement ceremony occurred in August, 2004. Chaplain (LTC) Tom Engle is far left and his wife is center.